Boomer Trek

One Baby Boomer's Surprising Journey from Secular Humanism to Faith in God

Bill Dunn

Boomer Trek
Copyright © 1997 by Bill Dunn

Published by WinePress Publishing
PO Box 1406
Mukilteo, WA 98275

Cover by **DENHAM**DESIGN, Everett, WA

All rights reserved. No part of this publication may be reproduced, stored in a retrieval system or transmitted in any way by any means, electronic, mechanical, photocopy, recording or otherwise, without the prior permission of the publisher, except as provided by USA copyright law.

Unless otherwise noted, Scripture quotations are from the *Holy Bible: New International Version.* Copyright © 1973, 1978, 1984 by the International Bible Society.

Printed in the United States of America.

Library of Congress Catalog Card Number: 96-61787
ISBN 1-883893-86-0

Dedication

To Mackenzie and Maureen;
my child and my child: so that you may better
know the deepest feelings of my heart.
This is me, this is what I believe,
this is what I want you to hold onto
when I'm with Him.
—Daddy

CONTENTS

1. Foundations Begin to Crumble 7
2. Boomerville 15
3. Baby Boomers and Church 21
4. Science Answers All 27
5. The TV Generation 35
6. Me, Myself and I 43
7. Sex and Drugs and Rock n' Roll 51
8. College Life - Bad Habits Ingrained 59
9. Yuppie Wannabe 67
10. Together on the Outside, Crying on the Inside . .77
11. Fatherhood 83
12. Conversion Completed 91
13. Is This Logical? 97
14. Wow! There Is No Other Conclusion 103
15. More Evidence - A Changed Life 113
16. Time - A Different Perspective 119
17. Politics 125
18. Not Afraid of Death .135
    Endnotes 142

CHAPTER 1

FOUNDATIONS BEGIN TO CRUMBLE

We were coming down the home stretch. Eight hours of Lamaze breathing, back rubs, ice chips and popsicles were about to reach their climax: the birth of our first child. I stepped aside to let the obstetrician and nurse do their jobs in that bright, sterile, high-tech delivery room of Yale-New Haven Hospital. However, the last thing in the world I expected was a deep and profound personal spiritual awakening.

I was just hoping the baby would be healthy and that my wife would experience as little pain as possible. (It struck me as strange then, and still does now, that a generation which absolutely glorified drug use in the 1960s and 70s would now become so attracted to the no drug, maximum pain, natural child birth technique. My mother, in contrast, swears by the Eisenhower-era style: knock me out, take the baby, and wake me up in a week or so.)

Everything went according to plan. The baby was born — a little girl!— and both mother and child were as healthy as could be expected after such an ordeal. We all shed tears of joy and let out a sigh of relief as the baby was letting out her first of many healthy wails. The nurse cleaned her up a bit and then put her under those french fry lights to keep her warm. (I half expected the nurse to shake some salt on her and then ask us if our order was "for here" or "to go.")

After bundling up the infant, the nurse laid her on my wife's chest. The baby quieted down and snuggled up as my wife held her tight. As I looked down at the scene, peered into my wife's eyes, and felt an overwhelming sense of love in that room, I was suddenly hit by a startling thought. As if whacked between the eyes with a two-by-four, I suddenly realized that the theory of evolution's explanation for the origins of life could not possibly be true.

Okay, I admit this was not your typical delivery room rumination, especially since I had not given the theory of evolution any thought since high school science class. But when I looked down at that darling little baby in her mother's arms, I realized something new. I instantly understood that it was impossible for her to be the mere result of some accidental, random, natural selection, genetic mutation, survival-of-the-fittest, biological process.

It was not pride or ego making me think this way. It was not some irrational feeling that somehow *my* offspring was unique and special compared to all the other births in the world. It was just a sudden realization that she — and the rest of us in that room, for that matter — had been designed and created. How could something as incredibly intricate and complex as human life possibly have come into existence by accident? I just knew that my daughter was absolutely, positively, designed and created by someone, or something, much more intelligent and powerful than a human being could ever be.

I was like a painting suddenly realizing that I was created by an artist (assuming, of course, that a painting had the ability to think). The mere existence of an intricate, marvelous creation argues powerfully for the existence of a talented and skillful creator. Living creatures could not have consciously created themselves. The evolutionary explanation that a random swirl of cosmic molecules accidentally came together as a living organism, followed by eons of genetic mistakes resulting in biological improvements, suddenly seemed, not only woefully lacking, but downright ridiculous. I mean, when you think about it, tornadoes blasting through junk yards rarely leave fully operational 747 jumbo jets in their wake.

At the time my daughter was born, I had never heard of King David or the Biblical Psalms. But the basic feelings he expressed in Psalm 139 were in my heart: "For you created my inmost being; you knit me together in my mother's womb...I am fearfully and wonderfully made; your works are wonderful" (Psalm 139:13-14).

I didn't know who, or what, created us. But I did know that he, or it, had done some wonderful works, and that he, or it, was on a plane of existence far superior to we mere mortals.

I sat there alongside my wife and new baby with my head spinning. I knew part of my amazement was due to the sheer emotion of the event. But my mind was also racing because of this stunning revelation that my daughter, along with myself and all other living organisms, were designed and created. We are NOT the result of some random cosmic accident. This attacked the very foundation of my religious beliefs.

At that time, I was a disciple of one of the fastest growing faith communities in the country. I had embraced the religion of secular humanism in my mid-teens and here, over a decade later, the fundamental assumptions which had been the cornerstone of my religion were suddenly called into question.

Of course, most people would say that secular humanism is not a religion at all. It is by definition the complete rejection of traditional religious beliefs and is often referred to as atheism. But please understand: everyone has a religion. People may not believe in God, they may not believe in Jesus Christ, but everyone believes in something. Everyone has a value system and a set of core beliefs about life and death which shape their attitudes and guide their actions. This is a person's religion.

As a practicing secular humanist I believed in mankind. I believed that there was no spiritual dimension to human existence and the concept of an all-knowing, all-powerful creator God was the superstitious invention of ignorant people.

I believed that mankind was the real god, and that science was our high priest. Biology, physics, chemistry, meteorology, geology, astronomy, medicine, and most importantly, evolution, completely explained all the mysteries of life. Previous generations lacked this knowledge, and out of fear invented those old religious stories. To secular humanists, armed with knowledge and reason, mankind was supreme.

As far as I can figure, there seems to be two major types of secular humanism. One group consists of optimistic, ethical, utopian people. These folks feel that if mankind uses reason, science, knowledge, and compassion, we can solve all of life's problems and create a heaven on earth. These are the kind of people who seem to gravitate to Washington, D.C. and are convinced that if they can just put into place social engineering program (and of course, raise ᴏᴜʀ just a little bit more) then everything will be wonderful.

This branch of secular humanism came from the Age of Enlightenment in Europe a few centuries ago. With all the technological and medical advancements since that time, they were really becoming convinced that the genius of mankind would soon bring the world happiness and contentment.

However, the faith of these people was somewhat shaken in the middle of this century when the combination of knowledge and science brought the world such "enlightened" developments as gas chambers, death camps, and a massive stockpile of nuclear warheads. It seems that mankind's science just might blow us all up before ever getting around to creating Utopia.

This allowed the second type of secular humanism to flourish. The followers of this branch of the faith don't worry too much about mankind's ability to solve the world's problems. Instead, all attention and devotion are focused inward. The key to this branch of the secular humanist religion is a constant and relentless pursuit of pleasure.

Pleasure-seeking humanists believe the same assumptions about mankind, science, and evolution as their optimistic utopian brethren. However, they draw the conclusion that since we're only here in the first place because of some random, cosmic accident — as evolution teaches — why bother caring about anything except fulfilling all of our own selfish desires? After all, as the saying goes: no matter how many years you live, you're gonna be dead a whole lot longer. So, eat, drink, and be merry.

Most people will notice that this form of secular

humanism is by far the most popular today. (I suppose you'd have to be living in a cave *not* to notice!) It is the philosophy that allowed the whole social revolution of the 1960s to flourish ("If it feels good, do it!"). It is the underlying principle which has caused so much cultural chaos in America these past few decades.

This was the exact branch of the secular humanist religion that I embraced during my teenage years. I pursued it as a loyal and devoted parishioner right up until that moment I gazed at my infant daughter, and realized my most fundamental assumptions about the origins of life were off base.

Becoming a parent was difficult enough to handle for a pleasure-seeking humanist like me. Most self-centered pleasure-seekers avoid even the simplest responsibilities whenever possible, so something as important and long-term as fatherhood was downright terrifying.

I knew in advance that my life was sure to change as a result of fatherhood, but I was certain — like all good humanists — that I was the master of my own fate. I knew that the changes in my life would be all my own choosing, whether they be to accept the challenges of fatherhood or to flee from them.

Now, suddenly, it was becoming clear that I was not at all the master of my fate. Some unseen, creative force was at work in the world. In comparison, mankind seemed incredibly small and insignificant.

On that day in the Yale-New Haven Hospital, I ceased being an atheistic secular humanist and became a theist. I was, however, far from happy or excited about this fact. I had little desire to meet this creative force (not being quite bold enough yet to utter the word "God").

Naturally, I was somewhat curious about the identity and motives of this force, but being the type who bristles at most authority, I would have been happy without any direct encounter. I had a sneaking suspicion, though, that I indeed would be confronted by him (or it) at some point soon. With that I possessed an even more certain and sobering notion that the events of my life were no longer under my control.

CHAPTER 2

BOOMERVILLE

Growing up in the late 1950s and early 1960s certainly was not a unique experience. In fact, my birth year, 1957, was smack-dab in the heart of the post-war baby boom era. There were more kids running around than you could shake a stick at. (If you don't believe there were a ton of people born during that time, just wait a few more decades when we all start to demand Social Security checks and Medicare benefits. It will be downright frightening, not to mention impossible to fund.)

My family was part of the great migration to the suburbs. All those small rural towns which happened to be within commuting distance of a city never had a chance. There was an explosion of new houses on new streets in new neighborhoods; there were new schools, new super markets, new appliance stores, new auto dealers, new everything. The American population seemed obsessed with making babies, making money, and buying every new invention to hit the stores. The country's attitude was: "We had to sacrifice all through the Depression and the War, so now we're gonna consume like there's no tomorrow." We baby boomers were the prime beneficiaries of that attitude and we grew up the most spoiled and pampered generation in history.

Certainly there were many people living in poverty during those years, we just never saw any of them in our shiny new suburbs. Few of the people I knew could be considered really wealthy, but on the other hand, the whole time I was growing up I can remember only one classmate who lived in an apartment. Every other kid I knew came from a family that owned a house. We were all solidly middle class. Even my dad, making peanuts as a school teacher (this was before they started giving teachers combat pay in the 1980s), could afford to buy a house and raise five kids. It was the golden era for going after the American Dream, and everyone I knew was going after it with gusto.

We baby boom kids, the recipients of all this prosperity, began to look at material comfort and security as our birthright. If the feelings of many adults who lived through the horrors of a depression and a war were that God's grace had shone on America, allowing it to survive and then thrive, it was totally lost on us kids. We thought things were always this cozy. We felt we deserved everything handed to us because we were special. Not by the grace of God, nor by good luck, nor by the sweat of our parents brow, just because we were special and deserved it.

Back in those days, long before Vietnam and Watergate made people cynical about being patriotic, we baby boomers were quite proud to be Americans. Unfortunately, it was not a "thank God we live in the beacon of democracy and most prosperous nation in the world" kind of patriotism. It was, rather, an arrogant, self-righteous "we're the best and if you don't like it we'll kick your butt just like we did to the Japs and Krauts" kind of patriotism. We deserved to be number one just because we were Americans. We were number one in automobiles, number one in TVs, movies, and radios. We were number one in atomic bombs. We were the best.

I can remember wondering how people in other countries could possibly live with themselves for not being Americans. Surely, I thought, children born and raised in, say, France would realize one day that they were not living in America and this tragic knowledge would just crush them. They would slink around their narrow cobblestone streets with baguettes under their arms and bags over their heads out of sheer embarrassment for having the terrible luck to have been born French. I really wondered why there were any people at all still living in other countries throughout the world since they could simply get on a plane and move here. (This was obviously before I had any understanding of such things as population sizes, immigration laws, air traffic control congestion, and most importantly, the fact that people from other countries were just as proud and pleased to be living in their native land as was I.)

But the main point was that we were number one and proud of it. We were Americans because we were the best; we were the best because we were Americans. The rest of the world could just take a back seat. We weren't lucky, we weren't fortunate, we weren't blessed from on high, we were number one because we deserved it! And we often applied this attitude on a personal level. Each and every one of us little runny-nosed baby boomer brats was the most special and wonderful person ever to grace the face of the planet. It was a feeling as pompous and as misguided as you might find in someone born into royalty, or even worse, a member of the U.S. Senate.

When we would see statistics showing how the United States, with five percent of the world's population, was consuming close to half of the world's resources, we weren't embarrassed or struck by a sense of unfairness and wastefulness. We honestly thought, "Great, we're the best so we deserve it. I wonder what we can do to push it up to seventy-five percent?"

A key concept we learned during this time was that material possessions will satisfy us and make us happy. This little notion didn't really manifest itself as a major problem until years later, but the seeds were planted.

The adults of that era had gone through some terrible sacrifices in the previous few decades. Having lived through the Depression and World War II they knew very well the concept of patience and delayed gratification. When the late 40s and the 50s turned into a consumer boom period, these adults joined in without reservation. It was the reward for all those years of sacrifice. We baby boom kids, however, did not have to sacrifice. We just sat back enjoying the fruits of someone else's labor and benefited the most from that consumer boom. It was the time when the most prominent baby boomer trait was formed: the instant gratification attitude.

A tidal wave of new products and services came to the marketplace seemingly overnight. It was a time of remarkable progress.

The most ubiquitous product, the television set, also became the most effective tool for a new breed of marketer to work his magic on the buying public. The technique of changing someone's feelings from "Isn't that product interesting?" to "I like that product," to "I need that product!" to "I CAN'T LIVE WITHOUT THAT PRODUCT!" is one of the key driving forces in our materialistic society; then and even more so now. Why work hard to invent a product which will meet existing needs when you can simply invent a whole new set of needs? It's a devilishly clever way to do business.

Because there was no overt threat of war (there was, of course, the nuclear threat, but this was so distant and abstract, either nothing would happen or we would be instantly vaporized and never even realize what happened), and because we had plenty of food, clothing, and shelter, we could really concentrate on materialism and pleasure-seeking. We did it well.

They say it is impossible to attend to a person's spiritual needs while they have desperate physical needs. In other words, you can't preach the Gospel to a starving man. Also just as true is the notion that you can't attend to a person's spiritual needs if they are so physically comfortable they don't even realize they have any spiritual needs. In other words, it is equally difficult to preach the Gospel to a man lounging in a hot tub, sipping on a strawberry daiquiri, and watching a big-screen TV.

This was the situation we baby boomers were in. Maybe it took us another couple of decades to purchase our first Jacuzzi or acquire a taste for daiquiris. However, the cornucopia of consumer products that were showered upon us and the notion that "things" will bring us happiness made it very difficult, if not downright impossible, for our generation to understand that we did have spiritual needs.

So the basic dogmas of the religion of secular humanism fit in perfectly with our basic attitudes about life. As the progressive elites in academe and the media championed humanistic views, we were more than willing to go along.

Ironically, most of us attended a church or synagogue

Boomer Trek

in our youth. The vast majority of baby boomers were raised in some sort of faith tradition. But it didn't sink in. We already had our god. We worshipped at the alter of materialism. Our shrines became shopping malls; our holy relics were our collection of credit cards.

CHAPTER 3

BABY BOOMERS AND CHURCH

Just as the last of the baby boomers were born and began growing up, the Supreme Court ruled that prayer in public schools was unconstitutional. Many adults were greatly offended by this decision, but very few of us kids really cared, if we even noticed at all. It certainly didn't bother me one bit.

As I mentioned previously, most of us kids did go to church on a somewhat regular basis. But since we were more concerned with materialism than with spirituality, church really didn't matter very much. It was just another part of our identity. For example, Frankie lived on Maple Street and went to the Baptist church; Jimmy had a brother on the high school football team and went to the Catholic church; Ralph's father was a dentist and they went to the Congregational church.

The church affiliation didn't matter very much in our homogenized suburbs, but at least most of us were dragged off to some church each Sunday. It was unlike the present generation where so many children (whose parents are baby boomers, by the way) are never exposed to a church service at all. They don't even bother pretending it may be important.

But as a kid, I was required to go to church and to Sunday School classes although I didn't really believe much of what they were teaching us. It all seemed a little too incredible to take literally. In my own mind, I put God and Jesus in the same category with Santa Claus and the Easter Bunny. They were nice little myths that parents taught their children, but no one with half a brain really believed it was true. I often got the impression that the people teaching the Sunday School classes felt the same way, too. Oh, there were some teachers who talked as if the Bible stories were a definite fact, but most of the other teachers discussed the Bible events more like folk legends: an Aesop's fable with a moral to the story. They never came right out and said the stories were bogus, but we could see that they were often nearly as skeptical as we were.

The Supreme Court decision reinforced what I was beginning to wonder: why bother with prayer and church and all that stuff anyway? It seemed like the most irrelevant topic I could imagine. Finally, there was an authority even higher than my parents who agreed with me. Although the Court didn't come right out and say, "all this church stuff is stupid," I decided, as a smart-aleck seven-year-old, that this is exactly what they meant.

However, looking back from the perspective of over thirty years later, I wonder whether the whole point of that Supreme Court ruling was less about their opinion on the separation of church and state, and actually more about their desire to impose a secular humanistic attitude of "all this church stuff is stupid" on the American people. Either way, at the time, I was glad we didn't have to recite prayers in school anymore.

There was one aspect of church, however, which made it somewhat worthwhile in my mind. I discovered that religious concepts were responsible for the existence of my two favorite holidays, Christmas and Easter.

Now, this didn't quite make up for all those Sundays in a row when I was dragged away from the TV set and forced to dress nice and comb my hair and be bored out of my skull for two hours. But in my mind, at least something good resulted from all this religion stuff.

Christmas was the birthday of some guy named Jesus, and Easter was the day our superstitious ancestors thought he rose from the grave. (We have to cut our forebears a little slack, I thought, since they didn't have the science, technology, and 20th century intelligence to realize resurrections simply can't happen.)

I wasn't quite sure how Santa Claus and the Easter Bunny fit into all this (they probably appeared in one of those obscure books of the Old Testament that no one ever reads, I figured), but I was assured that these holidays were indeed religious in origin. So I concluded that religion had as least a few positive points.

I held this opinion until I got a little older. At that time I realized that people who never went to church, and had no religious convictions, were still allowed to participate in the Christmas season greed festivities and the Easter ritual of overdosing on chocolate.

I was very upset when I discovered that church attendance was not required in order to receive Christmas presents and chocolate bunnies. This actually seemed more logical to me after I learned that the main reason we celebrate Christmas, Santa Claus, isn't even in the Bible.

(I remember a Sunday School teacher explaining this to us. I had always figured that all the great legends, Santa Claus, the Easter Bunny, the Tooth Fairy, Goldilocks, Jonah and the Ark, Charleton Heston and the Egyptians, David N. Goliath, Jack and the Beanstalk, etc., were all right in the Bible. It was confusing to discover some were not.)

The major impression I have about being a church-going person in my youth was that it was on a par with any other club or group with which a family might be affiliated. Being a member of a particular church was like being a member in the Elks Club or the Friday night bowling league. There were no long-term, eternal salvation aspects to it at all. We were developing such a short-term, live for the present, view of life, we couldn't even consider any long-range, far in the distance, philosophical questions.

The church you attended was simply something you inherited from your parents, like whether you were a Republican or Democrat. Someone would either be a Baptist or a Catholic or a Lutheran based on what their parents did. In the same way he would be a Red Sox fan or a Yankee fan or a Dodgers fan, again, based primarily on what his parents did.

Church was something that most families had as one of their many identifying traits, but to us baby boomer kids, it was way down the list as far as being anything important. We went through the motions and did as we were told. (This was before we were led to believe in the late 60s that open rebellion and arrogant defiance of authority were fashionable.) So we sat there each Sunday listening to some of it, believing even less of it, and developing a serious disinterest, if not a powerful dislike, for anything related to churches and religion.

But then a new age dawned (I don't mean "New Age." We'll get to Shirley MacLaine and her synthesis of ancient eastern mysticism and modern selfish materialism in a future chapter.) In the late sixties a cultural revolution was taking place which encouraged young people to question all authority and "don't trust anyone over thirty." After years of being passively obedient to our elders, it was time for the youth of America to revolt. (And trust me, we were *revolting*.)

Now, I'm sure I would have handled things a little differently if I had been 18 at the time rather than 12. I was a bit late for the heyday of counter-culture activities (a fact I now realize was an absolute blessing). I wanted to rebel and defy authority but it was somewhat difficult to accomplish at age 12. I had to settle for defying my parents in my heart while being polite and obedient in practice. Why? Because I wasn't willing to have my TV privileges revoked, or be booted from the Little League team or have my ears boxed for that matter.

One of the main messages of the counter-culture was that all traditional institutions were evil. As a seventh grader, I wasn't exactly sure what the Military-Industrial Complex, Wall Street power brokers, or banking cartels were, but I knew what traditional religious institutions were. I spent every Sunday sitting inside one. When the popular media eagerly joined in the questioning of the relevance of religious institutions (remember TIME magazine's "Is God Dead?" cover story?), I felt that people were finally discussing out in the open all the things I had been feeling in my heart.

What was the use, I reasoned, of going somewhere each Sunday if you hated it? People weren't forced to go to the Elks Club every week if they didn't want to. (Remember, I equated church membership with social club membership.) If people wanted to waste time listening to a guy in funny cloths ramble on about some old folk legends, let them. But don't force anyone else to suffer through it. Especially now that most intelligent people understood that it's an archaic old tradition. And as all the youthful, hip, world-changers had decreed: old traditions were obsolete and should be abolished.

My attitude stayed this way throughout my high school years. I didn't see any value in going to church and I really wanted to openly defy my parents by refusing to go. But even when I got the to point of being physically larger than my father, open defiance just wasn't a practical course of action. It wasn't that he would knock me on my butt (which he was still more than capable of doing despite my size advantage), it was just that somewhere deep inside I had this notion that respecting your parents was the right thing to do. So I clenched my teeth and continued to attend church each week, having to settle for shaggy hair and garish cloths as my way of being rebellious.

When I left home to attend college, however, that was it. I vowed never to step inside a traditional church building again. As soon as I was away from my parent's influence, I practiced my true feelings toward church: it was something to be religiously avoided. I was able to practice my true religion: secular humanism. It would be more than ten years before I entered a church building other than for a wedding or funeral sincerely looking for God.

CHAPTER 4

SCIENCE ANSWERS ALL

If there was a faint glimmer of hope in my mind that the lessons being taught in Sunday School might be true, it was completely crushed by the science classes I attended in the public schools. The overwhelming attitude of the scientific community was that here in the 20th century we have finally unlocked the mysteries of the universe. We have explained away all those ancient myths and superstitions.

Without actually coming right out and saying it, the message I received from my teachers was that all religions—Christianity included—were a silly waste of time. A belief in Jesus was no different than, say, some primitive mountain herdsmen sacrificing their toenail clippings to the enigmatic and wrathful cheese god. It was simple: natural science cannot find any evidence of a spiritual dimension to human life, therefore, it must not exist. (Of course, using something exclusively natural to find evidence of the supernatural makes about as much sense as claiming that a cinder block's inability to tune in a TV program is proof that no TV signals are traveling through the atmosphere.)

Certainly in our lifetime we have seen remarkable advances in the scientific disciplines. There have been tremendous increases in the knowledge and understanding of such fields as chemistry, biology, archeology, medicine, physics, astronomy, meteorology, pharmacology, and cosmology (or is it cosmetology? Well, either way, we've learned a lot).

There is no doubt that what we know about the physical world dwarfs what was known a mere hundred years ago. Some of the most remarkable discoveries since man first harnessed fire have taken place in this century. We've split the atom, successfully transplanted human hearts, found cures for dreaded diseases, created cellular phones the size of a deck of cards (the most useful of mankind's inventions—if you listen to the commercials), and traveled to the moon and back.

If any generation deserves to feel smug about its scientific achievements, I suppose it should be ours. I also suppose if any generation would feel tempted to discard religion and spirituality onto the ash heap of history along with other relics such as outhouses, wooden dentures, and blood lettings as a beneficial medical procedure, it again would be ours. I admit that I needed no extra prodding to completely dismiss everything they taught in church as foolish folk legends and embrace science as my personal god.

However, now that I look back, even with all this new understanding, from the vast expanses of the universe right down to sub-atomic particles—and everything in between—science has not adequately been able to answer two simple questions: How did we get here? And, why are we here?

It's not that science did not attempt to answer these questions. The answer they gave to explain how we got here was right to the point: Evolution. And their answer to why we are here in the first place was even more basic: There is no why; it was all a random accident.

As a gullible high school student I accepted these explanations without question. As willing as I was to believe that science had all the answers, I probably would have accepted evolution as a hard, cold fact even if it was presented to me as an unprovable theory. But it wasn't taught to us as a theory or a hypothesis or a supposition—which, of course, it is. Evolution was taught to us as fact; no reason to look anywhere else kids, this is it, the answer to all the questions about the origins of life. The one, the only, the super-colossal: Evolution!

Now, I'm not a scientist (but I play one on TV), however, I did get an "A" in that class, so I somewhat understand the main points put forth by the theory of evolution. It proposes that living organisms can and do change over time to better adapt to their environment. These changes occur when an organism is born with a random genetic mutation which just happens to make the organism better able to survive. For example, the mutation may cause the organism to be bigger, stronger, smarter, have sharper teeth, or be better camouflaged in color than its ancestors. Through the "survival of the fittest," this mutated strain of the species thrives while the old, inferior strain of the species shrinks in numbers. Eventually, the mutated strain is the only kind left and so the species has changed—or else the mutated strain is so different from the original that it is considered a whole new species.

The theory says that these dynamics are happening constantly, albeit very slowly, such that you would need a period of thousands, if not millions, of years to observe a major species shift. So, according to the theory, all living species are in the slow and tedious process of evolving into beings which are genetically different from their ancestors.

This explains how one-celled animals could have produced more complex beings, which kept on changing over time until they were furry little rodent-like creatures. They then produced a species of bigger creatures which later produced a species of monkeys which, in turn, produced apes, which finally produced human beings. All through genetic mutation and all by accident.

Now, the basic theme of evolution—that complex order can form out of random disorder without any outside assistance—is directly opposed to the Second Law of Thermodynamics. This universal law, which is readily accepted by virtually all scientists, states that any system allowed to proceed on its own always moves in a direction from order to chaos.

It can be applied to many situations. Think of the pile of leaves you raked and left sitting in the yard for a week. Did the leaves become more organized or more scattered when there was no outside help? Suppose someone bought a brand new car and put it in storage for 100 years. Would it be in perfect operating condition after all that time? Of course not. All its systems would deteriorate without any maintenance. Think of your child's bedroom. If you, the outside force, stopped insisting the room be regularly straightened up, what would it look like after a month? (I know, I know, it's too gruesome to contemplate.)

There have been two major motivations at work

during the last two centuries to explain why the scientific community has embraced evolution so passionately, and been so willing to ignore the Second Law of Thermodynamics. The first is that many people have a very strong desire to discredit the faith of their fathers. Charles Darwin, for example, had a horrendous relationship with his stern, disciplinarian father and took delight in attacking anything and everything that was held dear by strict, authoritarian Victorian society; including and especially Christianity.[1]

Since the Age of Enlightenment took hold in the Eighteenth Century, mankind has been committing the sin of Adam and Eve all over again: desiring to be as gods, knowing good and evil. An ideology which puts mankind at the pinnacle of all knowledge and understanding does not leave any room for God. Many people who have embraced science (myself included) did so because it glorified man rather than God. Evolution is the perfect theory for this frame of mind because it completely eliminates any need for God and places man at the top.

The other motivation behind evolution's rapid rise to prominence is the fact that science has the habit of taking a simple, sketchy, unproven hypothesis and accepting it as the one and only truth—until, at least, something more catchy comes along. And of course, the more impossible it is to prove or disprove a particular scientific theory, the easier it is to embrace it wholeheartedly.

It's like some of those archaeological announcements we occasionally see in the news. A team of Ph.D. earth scratchers uncover a fragment of jaw bone in some remote part of Asia, Africa, or South America. With that single fragment as the only concrete evidence, they then go on to explain every minute detail about this newly discovered prehistoric person. They can tell us the height, weight, age, and gender. They tell us how he died and what he ate for his last lunch. They tell us his shoe size, his VISA card number, how often he quarreled with his mother-in-law, and whether he was a tenor or a bass in the village barber shop quartet. All from a single fossilized bone fragment which, if you ask me, could just as likely be the jawbone of an ass. But the key is that no one can really refute any of these claims, and since they sound so scholarly and erudite, they are much more readily accepted; just like evolution.

Another strange quirk of the scientific community is the routine practice of simply ignoring any evidence which does not fit neatly into their pre-conceived plans. For example, in the book that started it all, *On the Origin of Species,* by Darwin, ol' Charlie himself was perplexed by the amazing qualities of the human eye, and frankly said so: "To suppose that the eye with all its inimitable contrivances for adjusting the focus to different distances, for admitting different amounts of light, and for the correction of spherical and chromatic aberration, could have been formed by natural selection, seems, I freely confess, absurd in the highest degree."[2] Funny, you never hear any teachers of evolution citing this passage. They just go on teaching that random chaos evolved into intricate marvels without a shred of intelligent design or outside help.

They also forget to mention the observation of Nobel Prize-winning geneticist, Dr. Francis Crick (of Watson and Crick fame, the discovers of the double helix structure of DNA), who acknowledged in his book, *Life Itself,* that "an honest man, armed with all the knowledge available to us now, could only state that in some sense, the origin of life appears at the moment to be almost a miracle, so many are the conditions which would have had to have been satisfied to get it going."[3] (Any chance that miracle of which you speak, Dr. Frannie, could have anything to do with God?)

However, back in my atheistic youth I was never made aware of the doubts these learned men expressed, and so accepted the theory of evolution as gospel. I assumed this meant I had no religious faith. But on the contrary, I hadn't realized just what a remarkable leap of faith I had taken. Of course, if I had spent ten minutes analyzing this thing I believed, I would have discovered something else. I would have seen that I was putting my faith in a premise so improbable, that by comparison, it makes belief in the bodily resurrection from the dead of a guy named Jesus look as ordinary and logical as believing the sun will rise in the east each morning.

As a cocky young high schooler, I was actually more religious than ever. And my new religion was science. To me it was much more logical than the old superstitious religion which was taught to me as a kid. This new religion used microscopes and computers as its tools rather than candles, robes and dusty old books. This new religion could expand your mind and increase your knowledge, rather than (or so I thought) hide your head in the sand and ignore the real world.

But most importantly, this new religion put mankind at the pinnacle of all creation. This was a much more ego-gratifying outlook on life than to think there was some omniscient, omnipotent, and omnipresent Being who controlled the world. I felt free with my new religion, free from the judgemental gaze of a wrathful God. My new religion, in fact, was completely free of all moral judgement. Nothing was moral or immoral; everything was amoral. The only laws that mattered were the laws of nature, physics, and chemistry. It was exciting, it was liberating, it was ego-gratifying, and it was dead wrong.

CHAPTER 5

THE TV GENERATION
(or Good-bye Values)

The invention of television is, as the saying goes, a lot like throwing a diamond into an outhouse. There is something valuable in there, but you've got to dig through a lot of filth to find it.

We baby boomers are the first generation to be raised right from the cradle with that electronic box of wonders emitting its magical blue glow in our midst. We proudly call ourselves the "TV Generation." We're not sure how to check the oil in our cars or balance our check books, but we know all the words to the theme songs of "The Beverly Hillbillies" and "Gilligan's Island."

It would not be surprising if archaeologists, uncovering the ruins of late 20th century America hundreds of years from now, conclude that the television set was the family altar of religious worship. Their research would show that the members of each household ritualistically gathered around this altar, which was usually located in the center of the largest room in the home. The people would spend hours concentrating on the holy icon, practically in a trance-like state. Many citizens even had mini-icons (13 inches measured diagonally) located in their sleep chambers. Presumably this was so they could pray just before dozing off, and then again, immediately upon rising. The archaeologists would more than likely write in their reports that this TV shrine was the spiritual and religious center of family life in what was known as the post-Christian era of the late 20th century.

Actually, that's not too far from the truth. Since so many present-day Americans have abandoned real religious faith, it is indeed the television set which nourishes the spiritual life of many people. Unfortunately, it is all too possible to be fed spiritual junk food.

Now I don't think that TV, in and of itself, is inherently evil. It's actually a remarkable invention and can be incredibly informative, inspiring and entertaining. It's just that such lofty moments are so few and far between. In the meantime, the TV viewer is bombarded by hundreds of less than enlightening ideas. The key to television is in its immense power of persuasion. The TV viewer basically opens up his skull and lets the ideas and beliefs of complete strangers come pouring into his head. This is where the power of TV lies: it can persuade far more effectively than any other medium. A thirty-second TV ad can motivate a person to hop off the couch and make a major purchase. The same sales information, if presented in written form (newspaper, magazine, direct mail, etc.), won't even stir a glimmer of desire.

The television has an amazing ability to make people covet. They covet things; they covet places; they covet attitudes and images. And we're talking good ol' fashion Old Testament coveting. That burning desire to possess something which is not ours, that craving for acquisition, that lust for having things which we really don't need.

TV is capable, in a matter of sixty seconds, of introducing us to an item we've never heard of, intriguing us with the prospect of some pleasure or satisfaction we might derive from owning it, and convincing us that we desperately need it and can't live without it. All in a minute. Is it any wonder that people get addicted to shopping malls and have credit card balances they can't possibly pay off even if they live to be 150 years old? Not to mention that most American homes have closets, attics, and basements which are crammed full of consumer goods (which were enjoyed for a little while but will likely never be used again). As a result, some people often make the decision to buy a new home primarily because they need more space to store all their stuff.

It reminds me of a discussion I recently had with a friend who was in the Army a while back and stationed in Europe. When he was on leave one time, he visited some distant relatives in Italy. They lived in a small farming village with no electricity and no running water. The houses were tiny, each with an outhouse in the back, and if the residents were lucky, it was not too far a walk to the community well in the center of town. He explained to me that despite the fact these people lived in what we Americans would most certainly call poverty, they had everything they thought necessary for a full life and were all quite happy. My immediate reaction, smart aleck that I am, was to remark, "Ignorance is bliss. They were too naive to realize just how bad they had it."

My friend explained that this was not the case at all. Many of the villagers were very familiar with modern life, having spent time in a nearby city. Some had gone to school in the city, some had moved there and worked for a while and then returned, and most of the villagers had traveled to the city for holidays or to sell their produce at the markets. They were not wholly unfamiliar with the modern conveniences we take for granted.

"I think the key is," my friend said, "that they weren't bombarded by television day in and day out. They were able to appreciate and be thankful for the things they had, instead of ignoring what they had and being obsessed about other things."

I think he is absolutely right. Television is the perfect device for making you forget that "a bird in the hand is worth two in the bush." In other words, it make us lose sight of how nice our situation actually is, including all the things we already own, because we're too busy coveting what we see on the screen each day.

Just think of the way television portrays how people should live. First off, everyone is beautiful. The only time you see a normal looking person (which is, by TV standards, downright ugly) is when a show needs a villain. Otherwise, everyone is tall, thin, gorgeous, and incredibly well-dressed.

How many American men spend each evening watching what amounts to fashion models appearing on TV shows and then when they look up from the couch and see their own wife who, for some strange reason, didn't quite have the opportunity to visit her personal exercise trainer, apply tons of make up, fix her hair, slip into something stunning with matching spiked high heels, and get breast implants during that two minute lull between cleaning the kitchen and putting the kids to bed, and think, "Man, the Missus is really letting herself go to pot." (While at the same time, of course, employing that males-only ability to be completely unaware of his own beer gut and thick crop of ear hair which more than likely would disqualify him from the Mel Gibson Look-A-Like contest.)

Also, on TV everything is exciting. Imagine if you could edit out all the boring and mundane parts of your life. I realize it would be silly for TV to waste 20 minutes out of a 30 minute program showing the star folding cloths, mowing the lawn, or cleaning a toilet. But when viewers are constantly seeing shows where boring moments are not allowed, they begin to expect that we all should be experiencing at least a few dozen once-in-a-lifetime thrills each and every day. No wonder so many people feel unfulfilled. Their expectations are unrealistically high.

Speaking of unrealistic, television teaches us that there are no consequences to risky behavior. On TV, no one ever gets pregnant or contracts a disease, despite a steady diet of casual sex encounters. (You never saw Sam Malone, the bartender on "Cheers," waiting in line at the health clinic for a penicillin shot or being sued for child support. In reality, how long do you think someone could lead that lifestyle without finding himself with a major problem? I've known a few guys who have tried, and the fun always ended rather quickly.)

Other unrealistic aspects of TV include the fact that cars always start on the first turn of the key, the star of the show can always get a parking space whenever and wherever he wants, and whenever anyone makes a phone call, the phone never rings more than once, and of course it's always the exact person the star wants to speak with on the other end of the line. No receptionist-trainees to disconnect or misdirect the call; no computer-run, phone mazes to waste half of your day. ("For customer service, please press 1. For sales, please press 2. For the name of a good physician to check your blood pressure because of this frustrating phone system, please press 3.")

On TV, people can be violently struck in the back of the head with a crow bar and the only thing that happens is they become unconscious for a few moments, wake up, shake their head, and then leap up and run to their sports car to continue chasing the bad guys. There is never any mention of traumatic brain injury, CAT scans, nausea, dizziness, memory loss, or the fact that a real human being would need many weeks to recover from such an injury, if they could fully recover at all.

Another aspect of television (and the movies, too) is the way religious themes are portrayed. For the most part they are simply ignored. No TV star is ever shown praying, or going to church, or reading the Bible. No one ever mentions, even in passing, the existence of these activities. Religion just doesn't exist on TV— for the heroes of the show, anyway. Sometimes religious people do appear on a TV show, but almost always in a negative light. Occasionally a story will involve characters who are either intolerant fanatics, fundamentalist bigots, or anti-abortion zealots. Once in a while a clergyman will appear in a TV program, but always as a bad guy: the slick, scheming, money-hungry televangelist; the evil, manipulative, sexual deviant priest; or the fat, ignorant, loud-mouth rural preacher.

But by and large, religious characters and religious themes do not appear on television. People who have faith in God and try to live according to that faith are about as common on TV as beer commercials emphasizing the fact that one is likely to get fat and stupid from drinking the product every day.

As a young man growing up in the TV age, many of my strongest values and ideas about life were shaped by the boob tube. I felt that the important traits a person should possess were physical beauty and a sarcastic, glib tongue. To be considered a success, a person should be wealthy, famous, and have an incredibly exciting career. From watching so much television, I assumed that all problems could be miraculously solved in 30 (or 60) minutes, good guys never die, and all businessmen are evil. I began to think we could eat every tantalizing food product we saw while never getting fat. We could drink every alcoholic beverage we saw and not get into legal or financial trouble. And we could be (should be!) sexually promiscuous and would never get entangled in an emotional web of unhappiness, not to mention contract a disease or face unwanted parenthood.

In short, by the time I became an adult, tens of thousands of hours of television viewing had helped shape my values to the point where I ignored all the qualities which truly give a person fulfillment and happiness: honesty, hard work, perseverance, loyalty, faith, and family. While at the same time I embraced those shallow and superficial values which ultimately lead to emptiness and despair: physical appearances, materialism, and self-centered pleasure seeking.

CHAPTER 6

ME, MYSELF AND I
(The three most important people to a baby boomer)

It is quite natural for human beings to be concerned with themselves. Self preservation is a natural instinct. We all want to make sure we are well-fed and safe. There is certainly nothing wrong with that. Even Jesus' teaching, "Love your neighbor as yourself," is based on the assumption that most people do love themselves and care about their own personal well being.

Baby boomers, however, have taken this natural instinct and elevated it to an art form. Our generation has made self-obsession and self-glorification the new national religion. The 1970s were labeled the "Me Decade" and the 1980s were labeled the "Greed Decade" in no small part because of the behavior of many baby boomers during those periods. And, of course, the Psychedelic '60s was the decade where all the self-centered attitudes of the baby boomers really began to bloom.

The anti-war movement, for example, has been

characterized in nostalgic retrospect as a grassroots quest for peace and justice. It was the movement where common citizens banded together and affected major policy change in the highest corridors of political power. This is partially true, but another major factor in the anti-war movement which rarely gets mentioned is the overwhelming desire of draft age, male baby boomers to keep themselves out of harm's way. To a generation as self-obsessed as baby boomers, concepts such as making the world safe for democracy, patriotism, and having a duty to one's country are almost comical. Keeping your own personal butt out of the danger zones is the only thing which is important. Communist hordes could have been ravaging Nebraska and Iowa, and many male baby boomers still would have been frantically trying to secure a college draft deferment (just not at the Universities of Nebraska or Iowa, of course).

If all the draft age Americans in 1941 had felt the same as baby boomers, our country most likely would have sat out World War II and at this very moment we would be overrun with German automobiles and Japanese electronic equipment. Oh wait. That happened anyway, but you get my point.

The other highlight (lowlight?) of the 60s was the social revolution which took place regarding sexual habits and drug usage. Noble terms such as "freedom," "enlightenment," and "liberation" were widely used to justify the new wave of promiscuity and narcotics consumption. Supposedly, all the harmful and guilt-inducing inhibitions of repressed, bourgeois society were being remade into a more open, carefree, and intelligent outlook on life. But that was, to put it delicately, a total crock. The underlying factor here was once again selfishness. Personal pleasure-seeking was the main motivation. From the consumerism of the 50s, to the hedonism of the 60s, to the introspection-to-the-point-of-being-silly of the 70s, and back again to the high-tech consumerism of the 80s, the baby boom generation has come full circle in its fruitless quest for selfish fulfillment.

I mentioned earlier that my generation has made selfishness the new national religion. This is actually very close to the truth. Since many people in the last three or four decades have abandoned traditional religion and do not actively worship God anymore, they have found a substitute to whom they now direct all of their worship: themselves.

The surge in popularity of the New Age movement, and the elevation of Shirley MacLaine to guru status, is evidence of this fact. Many baby boomers feel a spiritual longing despite all of their material wealth. This is understandable since all people have a spiritual dimension which must be fulfilled regardless of how vehemently the secular culture encourages us to deny it. But instead of turning to the true God who created the universe and everything in it and all His concepts of humility, sacrifice, and obedience, the baby boomers turn to New Age philosophy which, in a nutshell, states: I'm a god, you're a god, everything is god, so bow down and worship yourself!

The only thing new about New Age is the way they have corrupted ancient Hindu philosophy by adding BMW's, Rolex's, and high-yield mutual funds. Instead of helping someone to mature from their juvenile self-centeredness, this religion glorifies selfishness. Most baby boomers feel right at home with this concept. They simply broaden their selfish focus to include, not only all those physical and material objects, but also their inner spiritual life as well. Selfishness is not only a way of life, it has become a sacrament.

Now I personally did not get caught up in any of this New Age spirituality stuff. For many years I accepted the more popular notion that there is no such thing as spirituality. I believed that what people called spirituality was simply a misunderstanding of their emotions, which were, of course, bio-chemical in nature and nothing more than a result of our advanced evolutionary development. So once again I sided with the secular scientific community. Everything about us was based on chemistry and physics. As part of evolutionary survival skills, certain chemical reactions in our nervous system would produce feelings of fear, anxiety, hope, and love. Because of our advanced capacity to think and imagine (again, merely a result of evolution and chemical reactions), some humans along the way invented the concepts of spirituality and religion. Those of us in the scientific camp believed that this whole religion idea was a silly superstition which refused to die.

After many years, however, I came to a point in my life where I could no longer deny that I possessed a spiritual dimension. I knew that it was not just my imagination, or some brain chemistry-induced anxiety, or a case of heartburn, or some other scientific explanation. There was a genuine spiritual part of me that I had been ignoring. It was empty and it longed to be filled. Thankfully, when I was at this point in my life, a little paperback book appeared in my mailbox and introduced me to the God of the Universe and his son, Jesus. If I had met Shirley MacLaine first, there is a good chance I'd be, at this very moment, fondling crystals, worshipping my navel, and hugging trees.

I admit, I have been known to be somewhat gullible.

For example, I was convinced that mega-doses of Budweiser would make me cool and sexy, causing dozens of fashion models to gather around me, just like on the commercials. So, I could see myself falling for that New Age stuff — for awhile anyway. This is why after being introduced to Jesus I kept silent about it for a very long time waiting for the novelty of the "fad" to wear off. Only after my spiritual relationship with Jesus continued to grow and the undeniable truths of Christianity became even more apparent to me, not to mention the fact that my life completely changed for the better, did I muster up the courage to tell anyone else, no longer concerned about being labeled gullible.

But back before this happened, I sided with the scientific, non-spiritual folks. We certainly did not need Shirley MacLaine to legitimize our selfishness. The evolutionist, secular humanist point of view virtually demands that a person be totally self-centered. This is because one of the underlying principles of secular humanism is that all life forms have a very brief and finite existence. According to the scientific community, once we are dead, that's it. We cease to exist.

The whole concept of self-centeredness takes on a much more urgent tone. If we don't satisfy all of our lusts and yearnings now, we may never get the chance. If we waste valuable time sacrificing for others, then we have lost a precious opportunity to do something indulgent for ourselves. The question of who our ancestors were becomes irrelevant; who are descendants will be is meaningless. The only thing that matters to us is us, here and now.

When you step back and really look at this selfish outlook on life, it is very similar to the attitude and motivation of, say, a gerbil. Or maybe the annoying mongrel down the block who is always causing trouble with the other neighborhood dogs.

By accepting the premise that our natural, physical life makes up the whole of our existence, we unwittingly lower ourselves to the level of wild animals. And if you just look around and observe some of the behavior which has become so commonplace in the last three decades, you can see that this is true.

When your own well-being is the only thing that matters, when "do unto others as you would have them do unto you," is a concept that makes absolutely no sense because it is the complete opposite of selfishness, then conditions are ripe for situational ethics and relativism. With selfish secular humanism, God is removed from the equation. Right off the bat there is an absence of any absolute standards of right and wrong. Each generation can modify the rules of acceptable behavior to fit what it believes to be best for its particular society.

So despite a commandment stating "Thou shall not kill," which has been understood and respected throughout the centuries (this is not to say that it hasn't been broken countless times, but societies have recognized it as a just and proper principle), a nation can suddenly decide that it is now acceptable to rip a kicking, squirming, preborn infant from its mother's womb and throw it in the dumpster. And that there's nothing wrong with administering a lethal injection to Grampa if he's old and frail and taking up space and costing too much money.

While at the same time, however, a farmer can be subject to arrest and imprisonment if he attempts to cultivate his own land after some government bureaucrat has decreed that there *might* be kangaroo rats, or spotted owl turds, or who-knows-what-else nesting in the soil. (So much for personal property rights, eh?)

Or a parent can be arrested for using an age-old, tried and true method of instilling a proper sense of discipline and respect in his child by administering a spanking, which, these days, is lumped into the same "child abuse" category as beatings and torture as far as the social engineers are concerned.

Presumably, these elite secular social engineers who have dismissed God's version of good and evil are attempting to do what they honestly feel is best for all of society. (Without a firm standard of right and wrong, of course, they are doomed to failure.) But the sad irony of this situation is that when rampant selfishness becomes the motivation for most of the individuals in a society, even the supposed concern for the common good is irrelevant.

The social engineers can do all they want to try and build their version of Utopia, but most of the citizens in the culture could care less. They are consumed only with satisfying their own urges and desires. Unlike the social engineers, whose personal view of right and wrong has been modified, the general population has simply abandoned it. The only standard of right and wrong to a completely self-centered person is "if it pleases me, it's right, and if it doesn't please me, it's wrong."

This explains why our generation has seen such an explosion in substance abuse, greed, illegitimacy, materialism, divorce, laziness, adultery, abortion, frivolous lawsuits, and fraud. And unfortunately, the government has opted against enforcing the laws which were designed to keep people from sinking to this level. As a matter of fact, the government has abolished many of the laws which guarded against these harmful behaviors becoming rampant in the first place. They have decided that these behaviors are either the individual's "right," or a so-called disease which demands our fawning compassion. We, as a society, are not allowed even to frown on someone's actions, regardless of whether it's ruining his own life, the lives of those around him, or straining the taxpayer's resources.

The net result of all this is a set of societal norms which are darn near in the gutter. And I'm not very proud of the fact that my own personal values were right about at this level as I was becoming an adult. I was convinced that life was one big cosmic accident, totally without meaning. There was no God, there was no afterlife, there was no reason to care about anyone or anything other than myself. Therefore, the only reasonable course of action, given this particular view, was to seek all the things which gave me immediate pleasure and to avoid all the things which caused me any discomfort. This attitude formed the three major motivations in my life, the subject of the next chapter.

CHAPTER 7

SEX AND DRUGS AND ROCK N' ROLL

> "Sex and drugs and rock n' roll
> Are all my brain and body need
>
> Sex and drugs and rock n' roll
> Are very good indeed"[1]

I literally shudder to think that I once considered this pathetic song to be, not only an excellent tune (it's far from it), but also a wonderful philosophy of life. I should be thankful that I can even remember the song, I suppose, what with all the chemicals I dumped into my bloodstream during my youthful days.

From a self-centered, hedonistic point of view, the timing was perfect. I reached my teenage years and early adulthood at the exact moment in history when unabashed pleasure-seeking became the national obsession. The philosophies of the counter-culture had been gradually incubating in small pockets around the country during the early 1960s. Urban areas and college campuses were tuning in to the Woodstock generation mentality. Through the late 60s and then as I entered high school in the early 70s, the counter-culture became mainstream.

All of the messages I received during that time promoted a hedonistic outlook on life. It completely drowned out any message of temperance and modesty my parents, the church, or any other traditional source may have been trying to impress upon me. In fact, many of the traditional sources, such as the public schools and some church denominations, simply stopped promoting traditional values altogether. I guess they figured that being unfashionable somehow made the truth less truthful, so they simply went with the flow.

It's not as if the baby boom generation invented debauchery, of course. Other eras have also seen the allure of a "wine, women, and song" philosophy. It's just that the complete breakdown of societal norms occurred so quickly when the baby boomers came of age.

Many different mediums helped promote the message that rules were constricting and we should be a pleasure-seeking culture. Books, magazines, television, movies, advertising, and popular music all glorified the instant gratification way of life; especially the music. Rock n' roll was the music of our generation. I'm convinced that rock-style music is not necessarily evil. In fact, there are some devout Christian musicians and singers who can really wail. But the songs and the artists who were the most popular back in my youth (and possibly more so now) preached a constant message of "Get high and get horny."

The popular musical celebrities flaunted their own personal drug usage and promiscuity, and many of us looked up to them as idols and role models. For the most part, however, I really believe the music was following the culture rather than the culture following the music. In any event, we identified with the music; it was our music, it made us feel good, it helped us let down our inhibitions, and as an extra bonus, our parents simply hated it. It was a stark separation between us and the older generation.

When I was about 13-years-old, the Woodstock triple album was released. A classmate of mine who lived down the street owned a copy and I would go over to his house after school virtually every day. We would sit around and listen to the music — so loud that we couldn't even hear his mother screaming at us to turn it down — and stare at the photographs on the album cover. We imagined that we were actually there, sitting in the mud, getting high, having fun, being totally free. We longed to be a few years older so we could really participate in this fantastic new revolution which was sweeping the country. The 18- and 20-year-old kids were the ones who were really having all the fun. They were letting their hair grow long, wearing wild clothing, rejecting the up-tight values of the older generation, and living totally uninhibited lives. To us sappy 13-year-olds, it seemed so wonderful. We couldn't wait to join them.

With the philosophy that pleasure-seeking is the most important goal in life, it was just a matter of time before I had the opportunity to partake of the wild life. Soon after entering high school, I was introduced to my first ever mind-altering substance: beer. It was not very glamorous compared to Acapulco Gold, hashish, LSD, magic mushrooms, uppers, downers, or one of the other illegal narcotics, but it did the trick. It got me inebriated, swept me with a wave of happiness, and made me feel part of the in-crowd. It was also the beginning of an intense and rocky relationship with alcohol which lasted well over a decade.

Surprisingly, I was able to present a fairly respectable front during my high school years. I kept my grades up and participated in athletics. But it was the weekends and those post-game parties that I looked forward to with so much anticipation. In the fall it was the Saturday night parties after the football games. In the winter it was the Friday night parties after the basketball games. We would all get together and get drunk, smoke some dope, chase after the girls (thinking, of course, that we were the most suave and sexy things going, when in fact we were just a bunch of drunken slobs), and generally revel in our debauchery.

My high school years coincided with the time when the sexual revolution was really gaining momentum throughout the country. With the introduction of fairly reliable birth control methods (the pill in the 60s and legal abortion in the 70s), the sexual revolution promoted the idea that we could all now enjoy our sexuality without fear of pregnancy. Also, there was little to fear regarding sexually transmitted diseases at that time since the afflictions that were around were treatable and non-fatal. The dreaded AIDS virus had yet to be detected.

The sexual revolution turned out the be the biggest scam ever perpetrated by men against women. Using the subtle message that we can *all* reach sexual fulfillment by partaking of carnal pleasures as frequently as possible, men were able to dismiss the emotional and spiritual side of sex. As most people are well aware (despite vehement objections from the militant feminist camp), the sexual nature of men is much less interested in any emotional ties compared to the sexual nature of women.

A 24-year-old woman expressed it quite well in her reply to a 1981 survey on the change in cultural habits:

Sex and Drugs and Rock 'N Roll

"What we did when we freed ourselves physically was free men to live out their wildest fantasies of promiscuity and irresponsibility. Men never wanted to form commitments, but in the past they had to in order to obtain sex. Now that we women are no longer afraid of one-night stands, men don't have to commit themselves."[2]

The idea of casual sex without commitment sounded wonderful to me. The idea of getting drunk and high on a regular basis without any responsibility also sounded pretty darn good, too. And to do both with the throbbing beat of rock music playing in the background was the icing on the cake. This narrow, live-for-the-moment focus on physical pleasure and a complete disregard for any long-range consequences became my definition of a good and productive life. As the popular saying reminded us: "If it feels good, do it!"

Looking back on my teenage years, I am certainly not proud of my self-centered behaviors and attitudes. I suppose the urges I had were somewhat natural and not too different than those of most young males on the verge of adulthood. But the major difference is that most civilized societies throughout history have had built-in cultural barriers to keep the youthful male population from running wild. The United States, starting in the late 60s and continuing to this day, has for the most part abandoned these barriers. We, as a culture, are obsessed with self-gratification. We have glorified the individual's so-called "right" to do whatever he desires. Such concepts as duty, honor, delayed gratification, discipline, the common good, sacrificing for the future, rules of decent behavior, etc., have become quaint anachronisms.

Of course, as a high school student in the early 70s, there were still quite specific rules for decent behavior in my home. I could only partake of the physical pleasures on a somewhat limited and surreptitious basis. I made a conscious decision not to be openly defiant of my parent's wishes, realizing that free food, clothing, and shelter was a pretty good deal. If I had chosen to be an obnoxious and rebellious jerk and get myself kicked out of the house at age 17, having to suddenly provide my own food, clothing, and shelter, while having neither job skills nor job prospects, it would have put a serious cramp in my lifestyle. So I chose to play the game by being somewhat obedient and agreeable at home and then firing up all my hell-raising desires away from home.

There were times, however, when I didn't quite pull it off so smoothly. There were a few occasions when I staggered into the house many hours past my curfew and, if I had been sober, would've been terrified to see that my mom was waiting up for me. But since I was sloshed, I didn't really care and simply walked past her to my bedroom with a dopey grin on my face. I suppose she was too tired, not to mention very relieved that I was home in one piece, to have a loud confrontation right then and there. She did have a habit of rousing me out of bed extra early the following morning and seemed to take delight in "accidentally" banging some pots and pans together awfully close to my pounding head and running the vacuum cleaner in whichever room I tried to take refuge.

As far as I can remember (which isn't saying much considering how often I wreaked havoc on my brain cells), I only got into major trouble on one occasion. I came home late one evening with a stream of vomit splattered in a direct path from my mouth down the front of my new coat and onto my shoes. I feebly tried to explain that it had been someone else who had done this to me, but the physical evidence and the fact that my words were slurred, my thought patterns disjointed, and my breath laced with bourbon, convicted me in record time. I had to spend many days afterwards displaying heartfelt remorse. After a while my parents finally began to believe that I had been the victim of somebody "spiking" the punch at the party I had attended. (I neglected to inform them that the dastardly spiker was, in fact, me.)

All in all, I was able to maintain a fairly respectable appearance. To the outside world I was a well-mannered student-athlete who on rare occasion experimented with a beer or two. To myself and my close circle of friends, I was a self-centered, substance abusing manipulator. I'd do just about anything to get high, and say just about anything to have my way with a young lady. And during that whole time it never once dawned on me that what I was doing might be wrong. I had become convinced that right and wrong were what I decided they would be. If anything made me feel good, it was right.

Living under my parent's roof and having to attend high school each day forced a bit of temperance on me. I couldn't go completely wild. It would have brought a lot of trouble down on myself if I had fulfilled all of my desires wherever and whenever I wanted. This situation would soon change when I left the structured environment of high school and headed for one of our modern day Sodom and Gomorrahs: a college campus.

CHAPTER 8

COLLEGE LIFE- BAD HABITS INGRAINED

At the age of 18, I had developed a powerful taste for alcohol and, to a lesser extent, other mind-altering substances. I was convinced that promiscuity was the greatest thing since sliced bread and spent a great deal of time and effort trying to convince numerous females to think the same way. I thought religion was silly and any person spending time at church-related activities was a superstitious fool.

Despite these twisted values, I did possess one positive trait at that time: I had a reasonably good work ethic. Getting up early each day for school had become a habit and the regiment of six hours of classes followed by two hours of football, basketball, or baseball practice instilled in me a fairly strong sense of discipline. I may have had a tendency toward procrastination and being somewhat lazy, but my schedule didn't allow me to be an outright sluggard. I had to save all my drinking and carousing for the weekends, and so did not let it seriously affect my academic and sports duties. All this changed drastically when I left home for college.

As far as I can tell, the purpose of college is to give a young person the education and experience needed to succeed in life. There is no doubt many of my fellow students took full advantage of this opportunity and by graduation had indeed acquired knowledge and skills which serve them well to this very day. On the other hand, any institution that allows someone to do virtually nothing productive for four straight years and then awards him a bachelor of science degree would seem to have some serious flaws.

Now, don't think that I'm trying to place the blame for any of my problems on college. I take full responsibility for my behavior and any negative results. But the fact remains, a lot of hard-earned money was wasted so that I could have a nice warm place in which to hone my skills in the less-than-marketable disciplines of eating, sleeping, drinking beer, smoking pot, and chasing coeds. For me, college was nothing more than a privileged-class welfare state: no work, no responsibility, all the necessities of life simply handed to me without any strings attached. And for four full years not a single person voiced any objection to this arrangement.

Obviously, a college student is required to maintain a minimum grade point average to stay in school. If someone never attends class or flunks every exam, they will be asked to leave (or, it seems at some schools these days, offered a professorship.) But the amount of effort required to keep a respectable grade level was laughable. From what I hear, grade inflation and minimum standards have gotten noticeably worse in the last two decades. Today's college students look at my generation as the people who really had to *struggle* to get decent grades.

My typical college schedule had twelve hours of classroom time per week. Compare this to the standard 40 or 50 hour work week in the real world. Very few of my professors took attendance or deducted points for being absent, so you probably won't be surprised to learn that I was never in the running for any perfect attendance awards. I would estimate that my average weekly record was to show up for about seven or eight of the twelve classroom hours. (Physically present, mentally out-to-lunch).

I can remember at our freshman orientation being advised to spend at least two hours of study time outside of class for every one hour we spent in class. I suppose some students really did this, but it was completely unnecessary. In fact, for the first six week of each semester I would do zero work outside of class. When an exam was finally imminent or a report due, then I would have to invest a number of hours or days catching up and cramming. This was usually enough to get a "B" or a "C" and keep me eligible and on track to get my degree.

You must remember now, I don't possess some innate gift for learning things extra quick. I was of very average intelligence relative to the rest of the student body. The plain fact is, the amount of work necessary to remain a student in good standing was minimal. I would guess that even factoring in the few all-night sessions needed to cram for finals and some other last-minute panic studying, I averaged no more than two or three hours per day, five days per week, of academic involvement during my entire four year college career; and the majority of those hours were spent staring blankly into space while sitting in the classroom or lecture hall. I graduated with a 2.9

grade point average, one click shy of a straight B average.

I should also mention that the school I attended is well respected in the academic world. It is a small, private, northeastern liberal arts university with a reputation for turning out smart and talented students. I even received an alumni fund raising letter recently which cited some survey placing my alma mater in the top ten of small liberal arts universities in the entire nation. (I didn't catch who actually did the survey. For all I know it could have been the alumni fund raising department at my college, which seems to send me more mail than all the politicians running for re-election combined.) But I can only imagine what conditions must be like at schools with a reputation for weak academics and wild parties.

So, with this as the backdrop, with the need for discipline and hard work virtually non-existent and all of my personal core values focused on self-centered pleasure-seeking, let's take a look at my typical college day.

I would generally wake up sometime just before noon. Not counting my freshman year when I had to accept the class schedule given me (including one class that met every Monday, Wednesday, and Friday at 8:00 a.m., arrggh!), I was able to manipulate my courses so that all of the class hours were in the afternoon. The thought of ever again having to rise and attend an 8 a.m. class was perfectly loathsome. It was about as attractive a concept as having to work for a living. I usually would awaken a few minutes before noon, giving myself just enough time to throw on some pants and socks and stagger downstairs for lunch. I lived the last three years of my college career in a fraternity house (an invention of dubious merit, to say the least) that had a dining hall on the basement level. This allowed me to go prolonged periods of time without ever stepping outside. If the weather was lousy (or if I just didn't feel like going to all the trouble of putting on shoes and a coat) I would hole up in the frat house for three or four days straight.

After lunch I usually had a couple of hours to kill before my one or two classes for the day. I would hang out with my buddies and listen to loud music, smoke a little pot, and decide if I wanted to actually attend those afternoon classes. If I kept the dope smoking to a minimum, only getting mildly buzzed, I would most likely make it to class. If I ended up pretty well stoned or if someone whipped up a batch of high octane strawberry daiquiris, then I'd simply bag the classes for that day.

By late afternoon our impromptu party would be winding down and we would often go over to the field house to play some pick-up basketball, break a sweat, and clear our heads a bit. After showering we'd come back to the frat house for dinner and then be ready for the really exciting festivities of the day, the nighttime parties.

During the afternoon, it was usually only a few guys who would be hanging out and substance abusing. But at night most of the rest of the campus was ready to get together and have a rollicking good time. There was always an organized party somewhere each night. The day of the week or the time of year didn't matter at all (it could even be in the middle of final exams week). Between the fraternities, sororities, dormitories, and off-campus apartment complexes, someone was always having a party each and every night.

At least twice a week (and often three or four times) there was no need for me even to leave my place of residence. My fraternity house was one of the most notorious party spots on campus. (In my senior year the John Belushi movie "Animal House" was released and we kind of took that as a model for how we should run the place.)

Boomer Trek

We were proud of the fact that ours was the only fraternity on campus with cold beer on tap 24 hours a day, seven days a week. We even went so far as to take a vote to increase our monthly dues, insuring that we always had enough kegs of beer to back up this claim. (Possibly a foreshadowing of the concept of increasing taxes to fund a destructive social welfare program?)

We even assigned an underclassman the duty of checking the bar each morning to make sure the beer system was on and ready to go.

Friends of ours who were not members of the fraternity would occasionally stop by in the middle of the day just to check and see if our claim was true. They were never disappointed. Whenever they pulled that lever, even at, say, nine in the morning on a Tuesday, fresh, cold beer would come gushing out. If we had been awake to witness these surprise audits, which, of course, we never were, we no doubt would have raised a frosty mug to celebrate our perfect record. Any and all occasions were reason enough for a spur-of-the-moment party.

The main themes of each of these nightly parties were loud music, excessive intoxication, dancing, and the usual young adult mating rituals. It being the late 70s, where the ideals of the sexual revolution were widespread while AIDS had yet to rear its ugly head, I would be only slightly exaggerating if I said promiscuity was more common than studying on this particular campus. Most of the male students felt the proper thing to do was let their raging hormones run wild, and more than enough female students wholeheartedly agreed. Without getting into too many decadent details, suffice to say immorality and pure hedonism were rampant. It was also the era before sexual harassment and date rape became common topics. Few men saw anything wrong with these behaviors and few women spoke up.

The official parties would run to about one or two in the morning. Then smaller, private parties would continue on until three or four a.m. When I would wake up the following day there would occasionally be a pounding hangover to greet me, although in looking back, I am utterly amazed at how infrequent those hangovers were and how resilient my body was considering all the abuse I heaped upon it. Most of the time when I awoke I was back in my room, although how I got there was often a mystery. Occasionally, however, I would awaken on some strange couch or lying on the beer-soaked floor of some unfamiliar room and wonder "Where in the world am I?" or even worse, "Who in the world is this sleeping next to me?"

So this would be a typical day during the majority of my college career. By my senior year I was finally getting a little tired and bored with this routine. Unfortunately, I wasn't getting more mature and responsible. My tastes were just shifting to smaller, quieter gatherings rather than the wild multitudes which were standard at the big parties. Booze and drugs were still the main feature at these less boisterous events.

With only a few months left until graduation, many of my close friends became much more serious and concerned about the future. They were starting to clean up their acts, knuckle down in the classroom, and most importantly, actively work to secure employment by the time school was over.

I also needed to find a job, but my personal habits had become so lazy and disorganized that I did little more than talk in abstract terms about what should be done. I knew the real world beckoned and the free ride was about to end, but unlike a lot of my pals who accepted the fact that the party days were drawing to a close and, therefore, became much more responsible, I just could not get my butt in gear. Every time I would promise myself to get going — schedule some interviews, consult with a faculty advisor, write some letters, make some phone calls — I would instead end up having a few beers, forgetting the whole thing, and drinking the night away.

This pattern of procrastination continued through most of my last semester until I finally stopped promising myself that I would do anything. I admitted to myself it was futile. I was paralyzed. The four years of self-indulgence and irresponsibility had completely drained me of any ambition, motivation, or drive.

Graduation day came and most of my buddies had already secured an entry-level job or placement into a graduate school. We had one last wild party together that weekend, and then I packed up my brand new bachelor of science diploma and my sack of dirty laundry and headed home to my parents house, a twenty-two-year-old man with no money, no job, and no real goals other than to find someone who would buy me a beer.

CHAPTER 9

YUPPIE WANNABE

Coming home from college, unemployed and unmotivated, I moved back into my old room in my parents house. I was too busy whining about this cramped and restrictive arrangement to notice that it wasn't exactly a trip to Paris for them either. Raising five kids in a fairly small house was quite a feat, one that I, of course, did not at all understand or appreciate until much later when I started a family of my own. My parents had gotten used to the breathing room brought about by having a few of their offspring away at college. To have a 22-year-old man with a propensity for drinking and carousing until 4 a.m. suddenly set up shop in the midst of their happy home was quite a culture shock.

Luckily for everyone involved, the factory where I had worked the previous two summers was hiring college kids again on a temporary basis. They re-hired me for the summer months to pack and load boxes on their assembly lines. This was great news for my parents since I now had a steady, albeit tiny, source of income. More importantly, I had to be at work by 8 o'clock each morning which forced me to curb my night life activities significantly. For the most part, I also was pleased to be working and partially paying my way. (My parents have never, ever asked for so much as a nickel in room and board. I'm sure I could show up on their doorstep today with my wife and two daughters and they gladly would put us up and feed us indefinitely. Well, maybe not that gladly, but you get my point.)

If I honestly had my choice, however, at that moment in my life I would have much rather continued my college schedule: hang out all day, drink all night. I still managed to do a considerable amount of partying even with the 40-hour work week. When the 4:30 p.m. horn sounded, I would make a beeline for the nearest liquor store and toss back a six-pack as if it was water and I was a camel who had just trekked across the Sahara. Then, of course, on the weekends it was time to *really* party.

After about a month of this arrangement, a remarkable thing occurred. A couple of the bosses in the factory learned that I had graduated from college with a degree in business management. (See the previous chapter for a few dozen reasons why they should not have been impressed.) I was encouraged to apply for a production supervisor opening. They were actually pleased to hire a home-grown college boy as part of their "management team." I was thrilled for a number of reasons: I was sort of putting my college education to good use; I didn't have to pack and lift boxes anymore; and most importantly, I was suddenly making much more money.

The new job was hard work, especially being a naive 22-year-old suddenly having to organize and give orders

Yuppie Wannabe

to a department full of 30-, 40-, and 50-year-old laborers. I got the hang of it after a while and the new salary allowed me to move out of my parents house and rent a place of my own. I was settling into a routine and it appeared for all the world that I was a respectable young businessman. But my values hadn't changed a bit. I still thought the meaning of life was to seek as much physical pleasure as possible. Instead of spending the day hanging around a fraternity house smoking pot and chugging Iron City beer, I now had to spend the day in a production plant wearing a tie. But as soon as 4:30 rolled around, I was right back in that same frame of mind, drinking, smoking, blasting rock n' roll on the stereo, and trying to seduce the ladies.

My feelings about religion and faith were still the same. I was certain that anyone who spent time contemplating spiritual matters was a superstitious fool and was missing out on a lot of sensual enjoyment because of an irrational fear of the wrath of some phantom god. Not that I actually gave this topic more than a moment's thought, of course. I socialized exclusively with my own circle of pagan friends and let the holy rollers do their own thing.

When I first got the new promotion, I was afraid that the only people who enjoyed partying like I did were my blue collar drinking buddies. I quickly realized, however, that many of the white collar folks also relished the opportunity to get stoned and chase after carnal delights — they just happen to do it in a more sophisticated and subtle fashion. Even the older people in upper management, who didn't quite understand the drug culture attitude, enjoyed their gin or scotch and didn't hesitate to get pretty well bombed at various after-hour social events. The only unwritten rules were that you must never get into any kind of legal trouble which might embarrass the company, and you must never drink on the job. Unfortunately, I was having much too good a time to fully understand that these rules, unwritten though they were, were absolutely carved in stone.

Because most of my personal core values were geared toward doing whatever made me feel good, it didn't take long for some of the more shallow and superficial work place attitudes also to affect me. In the corporate management structure, there was plenty of approval to be garnered for anyone who "played the game." I certainly was looking for approval and wanted to be accepted by the people in charge, so I willingly played along.

The key to having this "right attitude" was to have a near obsession with money, status, prestige, and power. These were concepts which hadn't interested me all that much in the past, but since I had few firm values to guide me, I quickly got caught up in the success-is-measured-by-dollars mentality. Being young and at the bottom of the management ladder, by the way, was not that much of an impediment. Everyone understood that I was new and these things would take time. The important point was to assume the proper attitude. I could dress for success, speak using all the appropriate buzz words, and look down my nose at the lowly and vulgar blue collar employees. I started to get the hang of it rather quickly and enjoyed receiving approval from my haughty white collar colleagues. This was all taking place in 1980, the dawn of the yuppie era.

After working at this job for little more than a year, disaster struck. Because of increased production demands, I was ordered to work an overtime shift one Saturday evening. To me, Saturday nights were pretty near sacred. That was the peak party time of the entire week. I was very offended to be forced to work.

That evening rolled along smoothly and uneventfully. There was a skeleton crew in the plant and I was the only management person on duty. At lunch time, which was about 9 p.m. on this shift, a couple of my old blue collar drinking buddies asked me to come out to the parking lot where a cooler of beer and wine was waiting. I didn't even hesitate. Saturday night was my night, I thought, and maybe this is a way to take it back from those jerks who forced me to work. I sat in the car for about fifteen minutes, had a couple of drinks — not even enough to get a mild buzz — and went back into the plant. I finished out the night and forgot about the whole thing.

The following Monday at the end of my shift, I was called into the personnel office. They said there had been a report of me drinking in the parking lot during the Saturday night overtime shift. Now, I don't really know for sure what would have happened if I had categorically denied this charge. Maybe the evidence or the witnesses were overwhelming; I don't know. But I sometimes think that if I had insisted I was innocent, they would not have been able to do anything except give me a stern warning to avoid situations where "rumors" such as this could possibly get started.

However, when they told me of this report, I didn't think, Oh brother, I got caught! How am I going to get out of this one?! My immediate thought was, Yeah, so? It was Saturday night, for crying out loud. What did you expect me to do? My actual answer wasn't quite as sarcastic. I replied as pleasantly as possible, "Well, yeah, sure. I had a little pop or two. No big deal, it was Saturday night, you know."

They were noticeably stunned by my statement. I

quickly realized that they viewed this matter in an entirely different light than I did. The unwritten rule about drinking on the job had been violated. This time, they were the ones who didn't even hesitate. I was done. Fired. Finished. Kaput. Clean out your desk and hit the road, young man.

I was stunned. Unemployment. No more steady paycheck. Yikes! And I still wasn't sure exactly what I had done wrong. But I had much more pressing problems now. I had purchased a brand new sports car about six months earlier which left me with a sizable monthly payment. Also, less than a month before the drinking incident, I had rented a house. After scraping together the first and last month's rent and security deposit, I had nothing in my savings account. I could barely afford the car and rent *with* a job. Now I had no income.

I scrambled to get my resume up-to-date and set up some interviews. One entry in the classified ads vaguely described "management opportunities" and listed a sizable "potential income" figure. I set up an appointment and met with the owner of this small Hartford-based firm for a couple of hours. It went rather well. We really seemed to hit it off, although I wasn't quite sure exactly what it was they did for a living. Something about financial planning and investments, I gathered.

He called the next day and offered me a job. When he asked when I could start, I replied, "Put me on the clock right now, I'll be there in an hour!"

I worked at this new firm for about a week, mostly going through a lot of training exercises and being introduced to the other people in the office, when it finally dawned on me that what they actually did there to make a living was sell life insurance. All the talk about financial planning, investments, retirement strategies, etc., were just buzz words to keep potential customers from slamming the door in your face or abruptly hanging up the phone (or to keep potential employees from saying, "Whoa, wait a minute, life insurance sales? No thanks," during the initial interview, as I probably would have done if I had known). I was soon to understand that very few phrases can evoke a negative response in people quicker than, "I'd like to discuss your life insurance needs."

By this time, though, I was dead broke and decided to give it a shot since I was receiving a small paycheck (although it was actually some kind of advance against future commissions, an arrangement which I didn't really understand too well and which was to run out very soon). I convinced myself that maybe this could turn out to be a great opportunity. I was working in a fairly big city and was surrounded by young, energetic people. Many of my new co-workers were impeccably dressed, drove Mercedes, BMW's, and Volvos, and spoke in glowing terms about the fabulous wealth they were in the process of amassing. The atmosphere was noticeably more success oriented than even that of the management folks back at my old job in the factory. I wanted in on this success and figured that I could eventually get comfortable with constantly calling up strangers and selling them insurance. Sure I could, I thought, no problem. Especially if it was going to make me rich.

This was a true yuppie's paradise. Everybody talked the talk. Unfortunately, only a few could walk the walk. Of the approximately one dozen insurance agents in this office, only two or three were busting their butts and raking in the dough. The rest of us daydreamed and fantasized about being rich, but were too undisciplined or hung over or timid — or all three — to do the necessary work.

During this time I perfected my talent of being able to

put on a respectable appearance for all the world to see, while deep down inside having no real character or values to back it up. I still had my sports car, bought a few decent-looking suits and power ties, and abused my credit cards just enough to look the part of a successful yuppie. But I was constantly in a financial jam—late in making payments, owing money all over the place, and regularly hitting on my friends and relatives for a bit of assistance with the heartfelt promise that things were due to turn around any day now.

In fact, my income was meager because my work habits were atrocious — I was developing into the King of Procrastination — and what money I did earn was being spent on drinking, drugs, golfing, and other frivolous activities.

After a couple years of this, I married my high school sweetheart. This was the first time I had been inside a church in almost a decade, and it was the last time I planned to be inside a church, unless, of course, certain relatives had any say about where my funeral would be held. We settled into a nice little apartment close to my office with a surprisingly very low rent. This, combined with my wife's steady income, gave us a little bit of financial stability but also allowed me to carry on without making any significant improvement.

Pretending to be hard-working and successful on the outside but knowing that it was all a sham made me feel very empty inside. I was living a lie and it was affecting my self-esteem. My drinking increased. I started hanging around a couple of the cocaine cowboys who worked in our office. This being the glamorous 80s, cocaine was thought to be the ultimate sign of yuppie success. But in reality, besides being incredibly expensive, cocaine is emotionally devastating. It can drag a person down on a quick spiral of despair and disaster. In a way I was fortunate to be so financially strapped. I couldn't afford to get totally screwed up on the stuff. I was more of a party pest, occasionally coming up with a few dollars but mostly hanging around, drinking beer, and hoping other people would suddenly feel magnanimous and offer some coke to me.

I saw many people get thoroughly crushed by cocaine's enticing death grip. And if I think back honestly, I'm sure that if I had access to a lot of money at the time, I would have been crushed too.

My life was settling down into a routine of play-acting the part of a young, successful businessman, but in reality I was just drifting along, day-by-day, increasingly more empty, alone, and unfulfilled.

CHAPTER 10

TOGETHER ON THE OUTSIDE, CRYING ON THE INSIDE

After three years of working at the Hartford Insurance firm, or rather, after three years of having a desk at which to read the paper, do crossword puzzles, and daydream about being rich, I moved back to my home town. I worked a deal with an old family friend who owned and operated a small insurance agency. I would be the official life insurance department within his agency, and in return for having complete access to his existing home owner and auto clients (something a hard-working, professional life insurance agent would pretty near kill for), I had to help out with some of the routine office work.

It should have been a great set up for both parties. He would have an extra hand around the office when things got busy, and I had an entire wall of file cabinets filled with potential customers who had never been approached about their life insurance needs. There was only one small ingredient missing: a work ethic.

My old buddies at the Hartford office instantly realized this arrangement was a can't-miss gold mine. Obtaining qualified leads and having a ready-made introduction are by far the most difficult obstacles for any salesman. Those guys were green with envy and playfully asked if I'd let them borrow one of the many Mercedes I was sure to be purchasing soon.

But in reality, the only thing which had changed was the geography. I completely wasted the opportunity that lay before me to achieve financial success and security. My core set of personal values still emphasized immediate pleasure over responsibility and discipline. As everyone around me realized what a superb opportunity I now had to carve out a respectable living, I chose to dwell on how unfair life was treating me. While many other people my age were working hard, developing productive skills, and supporting their families, I was wishing I could return to my college days of constant partying and no responsibilities. I had taken to heart the mind set which defined the 60s generation and so many baby boomers: instant gratification.

I virtually dumped the entire responsibility for paying our bills onto my wife's shoulders. She wasn't earning a very large salary, but it was more than I was making and it was steady. I always had plenty of excuses to explain why money wasn't rolling in with my business: the economy was bad (it really wasn't at that time); everybody already had life insurance (not true, and anyway, how would I know? I only half-heartedly attempted to contact them); there's too much competition out there (what competition? I had half the town and a wall of file cabinets to myself); etc., etc., etc.

The more time that went by without any positive results at my new business arrangement, the more depressed I got. I became immobilized. I knew what I should be doing, but I just could not make myself get it in gear. As I became more and more depressed, my main motivation each day was to take the emotional pain away. I retreated into the soothing, take-the-easy-way-out world of getting intoxicated. The pain of being responsible, the pain of being an adult, the pain of failing at my golden business opportunity was simply overwhelming me.

I still kept up the appearance of being successful and hard-working. I continued to dress nicely in suits and ties; I used all the proper buzz words and phrases; I talked excitedly about all the lucrative projects I was working on. But it was a false front. When I would announce that I had an important appointment and needed to leave the office, more often than not I would drive straight to my favorite tavern, park directly behind the building so no one could see my car, and spend the rest of the afternoon drowning my sorrows at the bar.

Years later, I discovered that the particular skills and talents needed to be a successful self-employed insurance agent have never been my strong suit. There are certain tasks and occupations to which I am much better suited. I didn't realize it at the time, but I was trying to fit my round peg of ability into a square hole of vocation. In other words, even if I was sober and motivated, I sincerely doubt I would have become anything more than mediocre in that business. Of course, at that point in time, mediocre financial results would have been greatly welcomed.

But I didn't understand myself very well at the time. Heck, I didn't understand much of anything at the time, except that I was unhappy and there were only two old pals who could bring a smile to my face: Buddy Weiser and Vodka N. Tonic.

Unfortunately at this time, I had no virtuous values

either to inspire me to be more successful or to guide me towards a more suitable career. I had no self-discipline, courage, wisdom, perseverance, or faith; especially faith. Being an atheistic secular humanist made things all the more despairing. I was sure life itself had no ultimate meaning and, therefore, the only logical goal I could have was to seek personal pleasure as often as possible and for as long as possible.

It's been said that for a true atheist, the only real question about his life is when and how to commit suicide. After all, to an atheist, human beings are the same as eggplants, only slightly more complex genetically. We're just another random life form which happened to appear on this earth; we live for a painfully brief time; and then upon death we become food for other life forms. That's it. There's nothing more meaningful about human life than that.

Human beings do have a small degree of control over this brief period of living, which, as far as I can tell, eggplants do not enjoy. (Anyone from the Eggplant Institute of America can feel free to correct me on this one.) Therefore we are faced with many choices about the way we can live out our existence. But since our ultimate fate is always the same — a tasty snack for the graveyard worms — these choices often focus on short term attempts to minimize the day-to-day pain and anxiety of life.

This is especially true if a person's emotional development has been stunted. A widely-held view in the field of addiction research concludes that emotional growth ceases to develop at the time when people become immersed in their particular addiction. Whether drugs, alcohol, gambling, abusive relationships, etc. (mine, of course, was booze), the emotional stability of the addicted person remains locked at that one, immature level. So, for me, even though I was only a few years away from turning 30, my emotional development was at about age 16 and holding.

This probably explains why I refused to accept adult responsibilities and had such a negative view of life. In fact, I was certain that life was one big cruel joke. The familiar bumper sticker and T-shirt slogan, "Life [Stinks] and Then You Die," was a profound philosophical analysis of the human condition as far as I was concerned.

I was astute enough to understand that my situation — drinking too much, working too little, and all the while wishing I was a financially successful yuppie — could not continue. Somehow, somewhere, I needed to start earning more money. Either that, or I needed to dump my financial responsibilities along with any pretense about being a respectable citizen. Both of these options were pretty depressing since they meant I either would have to work much more and drink much less, or I would have to abandon my wife, house, and car and live in a flophouse somewhere.

The first option, spending the majority of my waking hours working hard and earning more money, was simply something I did not want to do. The second option, living in a flea-infested hovel with a bunch of other winos, was actually the more attractive scenario at that point in my life. (I figured it wouldn't be all that different from the fraternity house I had lived in for three years.)

Whenever I would see the stack of unpaid bills piling up and that pleading look in my wife's eyes of, "When? When are things going to get better?" I would honestly start toying with the idea of just taking off. Pack a small bag, jump on a Greyhound bus, and disappear forever. Go somewhere, anywhere — Florida or Oregon or anyplace in between — where nobody knew me and then collect welfare checks and remain as drunk as possible until this miserable life was finally over. (Some atheists make their suicide decision with a dramatic bang; apparently I was leaning more toward a slow and hazy fade out.)

    I never came really close to making such a drastic move, but the idea popped into my head often enough. If it ever had happened, I definitely would have had to move to a different part of the county. I never could have collected government assistance in the same area where all my relatives resided. If there's one thing my family has a firm handle on, it's the difference between the deserving poor and the undeserving poor. Their World War II era work ethic is simple: any able-bodied person who chooses to let the taxpayers support him rather than get his butt in gear is the lowest of low lifes. If I had decided to use assistance checks as the funding for drinking myself to death right in my own home town, my relatives probably would have dragged me by my hair to the nearest Marine recruiting office. I'd have been a Greyhound bus all right, but one heading straight for Parris Island.

    But thankfully it never reached that point. Besides, my attention was soon distracted from all these thoughts of feeling sorry for myself by a sobering announcement: my wife was pregnant. Suddenly a stark choice was staring me in the face and demanding that I make a decision. I could either run away from all my responsibilities, including a soon-to-appear helpless infant, or I could stay and accept my obligations like an adult.

CHAPTER 11

FATHERHOOD

During the entire time my wife was pregnant, every person I met felt a duty to remind me that life would soon be completely changed. Friend and stranger alike took delight in explaining in detail how virtually every facet of human existence — eating, sleeping, entertainment, finances, traveling, socializing, etc.— would be totally altered once the baby was born. I'm still not sure whether this was done out of a concern that I be well-informed and educated about parenthood, or simply out of a sadistic desire to watch my jaw hang open in terror as they expounded on and on and on. No one actually used the words "prison sentence," but that seemed to be the general picture many of them were painting.

In fact, it turned out that all theses dire warnings about drastic change barely scratched the surface. I guess a person simply has to live through certain events to comprehend them fully. The verbal descriptions, it seems, only sketched a vague and shadowy outline. One must experience a string of sleep-interrupted nights to appreciate the full effect. Just as one must experience the maddening daily routine of taking two-and-a-half hours to pack approximately 150 pounds of "baby gear" into the car just to go on a ten minute drive across town.

Ironically, all of these changes — so much more momentous than I had imagined — were not really terrible at all. Something deep within me, a feeling which had sat dormant during my first 27 years of life, came to the surface. I can describe it only as some sort of melding of the concepts of duty, responsibility, and commitment. For possibly the first time in my life, I suppressed my selfish instinct and put some other interest first. The well-being of my little daughter was now actually more important to me than my own well-being.

To many people this kind of caring and responsibility is nothing new. But to a self-absorbed baby boomer such as myself, it was more of a startling change than all the lack of sleep and auto travel preparations combined.

For the first time in my life, I could appreciate the idea of someone giving up his life for someone else. Up until then, I was convinced there was absolutely nothing worth dying for; not king, nor country, nor mother, nor brother, nor wife. Self-preservation was my highest ideal. If faced with the choice between any one of them or me, I would always choose to protect me. (A strange and paradoxical point of view, actually, for someone so convinced that life was a random, meaningless joke, and who was well on the way to drinking himself to death.)

But now, with this new little baby in the world, I could say without hesitation — and really mean it — that I

Fatherhood

would throw myself in front of a bus to save her life. Frankly, it was a very weird sensation to care so much about someone other than myself for a change.

The other weird sensation which came with parenthood was the result of the delivery room revelation that the theory of evolution did not adequately explain the origins of human life. After accepting the theory as gospel truth in high school and using it as the foundation of my naturalistic, humanistic, atheistic view of the world, I gave the theory very little subsequent thought. (I mean, really, how often does the topic of Darwinian natural selection come up for discussion at a Sunday afternoon keg party to watch football games on TV? "Holy Cow! Did you see that catch, Freddie?!" "Yup, it was a dandy, Billy Boy, but you know sumthin', I just don't feel comfortable with the notion that random genetic mutations can cause improvements to a particular species. How 'bout you?" "Uh, Fred, maybe you oughta switch to root beer for a while, OK?")

But then I witnessed the miracle of birth and was overwhelmed by the eerie sensation that there had to be some kind of superhuman creator in the universe. I started running the basics of Darwin's hypothesis through my mind again, and this time, unlike in high school, I realized the theory was rife with unanswered questions.

Now, I *will* grant that the theory of evolution just may explain how very simple organisms might have been able to change over the millennia. But I began to lose faith in the idea that highly developed, genetically intricate beings can have a chromosomal mutation — in other words, have something go very, very wrong — which subsequently produces positive results.

If modern science has taught us anything, it is that when a complex system has one of its components go out of kilter, the system is inevitably changed for the worse. In biological terms, when an organism is produced with a genetic mutation, it is either vastly inferior to the parent organism or, much more likely, unable to survive at all. It is as if a component suddenly breaks inside my black-and-white TV. What scenario is more probable: that my black-and-white TV is now inoperable, or that it is suddenly a color TV? The theory of evolution is on a par with believing it is possible that my TV — on its own, just by accident — can become color. The whole theory is base upon the assumption that an error, a random mistake occurring in a sophisticated, highly-tuned organism will produce, not disability or death, but a major improvement. It started to dawn on me that this was incredibly unlikely.

Even if this part of the theory of evolution was true, that organisms could randomly mutate and produce vastly different and superior progeny, it still does not explain how living organisms came into being in the first place. Remarkably, the secular, naturalistic, non-God proponents accept without a second thought the notion that life began on this planet wholly by accident. I know that I did.

I wholeheartedly embraced the explanation that countless eons ago clouds of gases — hydrogen, oxygen, nitrogen, carbon, and whatever else compose the building blocks of life — were swirling about without a shred of outside guidance. They were obeying only the law of physics. One day some of these atoms banged into each other and, totally by luck, formed a new kind of molecule. Then these molecules continued to match up and expand and become more complex — accidentally. Then the molecules found themselves arranged — accidentally — in that extremely complex double helix pattern of which D.N.A. strands are composed. Finally, the molecules reached a point where — Shazzam! — they accidentally became a living, one-celled organism capable of not only taking in necessary nutrients and expelling waste products to sustain its own life, but also capable of reproducing an exact replica of itself. (Oh, and did I mention that it all happened by accident?)

Then at this point, the natural selection process took over and the organism mutated and changed and became more sophisticated. It branched off into new species and over the course of a billion-gazillion years produced such diverse and bizarre living organisms as a rose, an aardvark, a sperm whale, and Larry King — all by random accident.

It sounded good to me back in high school, as long as I didn't think to deeply about it. And best of all, it put mankind at the pinnacle of intelligent existence, thereby eliminating any need for God. It was the perfect way of viewing the world if you were a self-absorbed, smart-aleck seventeen-year-old.

So a decade later, completely by surprise, I was faced with the disturbing thought that the fundamental assumptions which had guided my understanding of the universe were seriously flawed. And not only that, it was beginning to appear that something much more intelligent and awesome than mankind existed in the universe, some unfathomably powerful designer and creator of life.

I felt uncomfortable for two reasons: first of all, it was frustrating to realize that I had been thinking and acting based on false assumptions for so many years. It was as if I had been playing baseball thinking that the object of the game was to avoid making contact with the pitch (which is, come to think of it, a lot like the way I played the game in college). Secondly, the idea that there was something much more intelligent than mankind raised my prideful ire. I had very much enjoyed the notion that I, or at least my species, was the ultimate repository of knowledge and wisdom. If there was something capable of creating man — and so by definition infinitely more intelligent — then we were not that impressive after all.

My pride was wounded by this new understanding. I didn't like the idea of being wrong all those years, and I *really* didn't like the idea of being part of a vastly inferior species. It had not occurred to me yet that this awesome creator might have made us with some wonderful purpose in mind. I did not realize that this creator might be capable of communicating with us and thus enriching our lives. And it certainly had not dawned on me that it may be possible for us to live forever if we follow the ways of this creator. I was just plain ol' sore about the whole thing and wished I never knew about it.

I tried for a while to ignore it; to pretend that I really didn't have this new knowledge. But it just would not work. I was kind of like those anti-nuclear activists who so desperately wish that mankind had never learned how to split the atom, they think by pleading with the world to dismantle all the bombs and then pretend that no one knows how to build any more, we can really have a nuke-free planet. Of course, I shudder just as much as the next guy at the thought of a device the size of a suitcase being able to vaporize Manhattan, but I also realize that once we acquired that knowledge back in 1945, it was impossible to unlearn it.

For a while just after my daughter was born, I tried to unlearn the knowledge that a supernatural power had designed and created mankind, but it was no use. Finally after months of struggling, I glumly gave up and accepted the fact. Luckily, it didn't take too much longer for my fear of the unknown and my wounded pride to subside, and for my curiosity to become aroused. I started to wonder about him — or it. Who? What? Why? Where? When?

How? I figured knowledge was better than ignorance (which had not exactly been my standard approach in life up until this point), so I decided that if it was possible to learn anything specific about this, this...*force,* I should learn it.

There was, however, one very uncomfortable thought which kept popping into my head. With greater and greater frequency I kept asking myself, "Could it possibly be that what they taught me in Sunday School twenty years ago is...is *true*?!!"

To an avowed, cynical, hedonistic atheist, the idea that traditional Judeo-Christian monotheism accurately explained the relationship between the human race and its creator was almost as stunning as the original hospital room revelation that man was not the supreme being. I was in for many more surprises.

CHAPTER 12

CONVERSION COMPLETED

I was not in a very good mood that evening. It was the week between Christmas Day and New Year's, and the holiday season was proving to be more depressing than ever. I had no inkling of the fact that it was about to be my spiritual birthday.

Since childhood I had always felt a bit of a letdown immediately following Christmas. All that wondering, all that anticipation, all that unabashed greed as I envisioned the marvelous gifts I hoped to receive, would build up for at least a month. Then suddenly, in the blink of an eye, it was over. Regardless of whether I received nice gifts or not (I usually did), I would feel depressed. I felt there was now nothing to look forward to except a few more days of vacation and then back to school or work and three long months of dreary winter. It was a post-Christmas attitude which was formed in childhood and carried over intact into my adult life.

On top of the seasonal blues, I had some other alarming pressures hanging over my head that year: new parental responsibilities and serious financial woes.

Our infant daughter was now eight months old and an absolute joy, to be sure, but also very expensive. It's amazing, for example, how a little snow suit with less than one-tenth the fabric of my own winter coat could possibly be the same price. Or how a $12 sack of disposable diapers would need to be replaced seemingly every twenty minutes. Or how those little jars of baby food with half a mouthful of green mush inside could cost so darn much. The bills were piling up and there was little relief in sight.

My insurance salesman job was, as I mentioned in a previous chapter, a major problem. Or, more accurately, the way I did the job was a major problem. Earning money solely on a commission basis can be quite lucrative for someone with drive and determination. Unfortunately, I had neither. My desire to become rich and famous using the procrastination method of selling ("Yup, by golly, I'm gonna call on that potential customer...first thing next week!") was proving to be a disaster.

So, already feeling depressed because of the holiday season and realizing that December was going to be my worst sales month ever, I followed my tried and true motto: "When the going gets tough, the tough get drunk." It was a quick and easy answer which never failed to make all my troubles disappear — at least until the morning.

I opened the refrigerator and gasped in horror. There was only one beer left! I frantically spun around and looked at the clock: 8:05 p.m. Ugh! The liquor stores had just closed (including the one that would accept my personal check and then hold it for a week) and I had promised my wife I wouldn't go out to a bar that evening. This was an easy promise to make since I only had about seventy-five cents in my pocket. I couldn't believe my bad luck. I had no way of drowning my sorrows.

I slumped onto the couch, nursing that one precious beer and grabbed the TV Guide. Rats! Not even a good ball game on the tube that night, either.

As I sat there feeling sorry for myself, I noticed a paperback book on the coffee table which had recently come in the mail. It was entitled *Power for Living*.[1] I vaguely remembered that there had been an ad on TV featuring Janet Lynn the figure skater and Julius Erving the basketball star offering the book. I thought they were talking about a new energy-enhancing diet for athletes, or something like that, but they did say the book was absolutely free and gave an 800 number. Since I'm the kind of guy who would probably call and order a bucket of boogers as long as it had an 800 number and was free, I had placed a call, not having any idea what the book was about. I forgot all about it in the month or so it took for the book to arrive.

So on this cold and depressing evening, having nothing else to do, I sat back on my couch and started reading the book. After the first few pages I realized that the book discussed spirituality and God. Well now, I thought, these are some of the same ideas which have been bugging me ever since my daughter was born eight months earlier. Maybe the author of this book could shed a little light on the subject.

The book talked about the frustration and emptiness of trying to live your life alone, without the power of God to help. To this day, well over a decade later, I can vividly remember thinking to myself, "What is this guy, a mind reader? He's describing exactly how I feel!"

I was convinced that there had to be some kind of supernatural God — the existence of complex life was ample proof of an almighty creator — but I had no idea if we were able to have any present-day contact with him — or it. The idea that we could receive help and guidance from God excited me.

Then the book explained some spiritual laws of the universe. The first was that God loves us and has a wonderful plan for our lives. I found that thought very comforting since, except for my immediate family, the cold, cruel world was making me feel decidedly unloved of late.

The next law was that all people are sinful and separated from God. Since it discussed how all people have fallen short and not just me specifically, I didn't take offense. Being singled out for criticism was something I didn't handle well at all (most insecure people don't). But I let my guard down a little that evening and admitted, OK, maybe I had done something wrong once or twice during the previous 27 years. (Or more likely, once or twice every 30 seconds during the previous 27 years.)

The third law was that Jesus Christ is God's only provision for mankind's sin. Hmm, where have I heard that before? It might have been in sixth grade Sunday School class, but I was too busy throwing spitballs or staring out the window to have paid much attention.

The book explained that God loved his creation so much that he couldn't stand to see us separated from him. Therefore, he sent a part of himself to become a human being to bridge the gulf between us.

The last spiritual law stated that we must individually receive Jesus Christ as Savior and Lord. In this way we can know and experience God's love and plan for our lives. The book explained that receiving Christ is simple and painless and whoever does it should expect tremendous changes to take place in his or her life.

The baby was finally asleep and my wife, quite tired

herself, said good night and went to bed. I was alone in the living room.

I sat there on the couch thinking, "Do I want tremendous changes to take place in my life?" The immediate answer was that I *needed* tremendous changes in my life. The bill collectors would be forcing change upon me soon, not to mention that my brain cells and my liver weren't going to hold out forever.

I sat back, took a deep breath, and closed my eyes. Man, the guy who wrote this book honestly believes that everything they tried to teach me in Sunday School twenty years ago is really true. And he wants me to believe that it is true, too. Well, a lot of the ideas and values that I've been following these past couple decades have turned out to be much less than advertised, so maybe the guy with this funny little paperback knows what he's talking about. I decided it was right.

I picked up the book and read the short prayer. Then I opened my heart and *prayed* the short prayer, attempting to sincerely communicate with God for the first time in my adult life:

"Dear God, I've been living my life my own way. Now I want to live it your way. I need you and I am now willing for you to take control of my life. I receive your son Jesus Christ, as my personal Savior and Lord. I believe He died for my sins and has risen from the dead. I surrender to Him as Lord. Come, Lord Jesus, and occupy the throne of my life. Make me the kind of person you want me to be."[2]

I sat back on the couch and sighed. OK, that was kind of weird but it certainly wasn't too bad. Some doubt was already creeping into my mind, but I had to admit, during those moments when I was praying I really believed it was true. Whether a divine revelation or simply out of desperation, I had really believed it.

I looked around the quiet room. Nothing noticeable was occurring. There were no bells and whistles or beams of light shining down from the clouds into my living room. I just sat there for a few minutes feeling peaceful. I looked at our Christmas tree and thought for the first time in three weeks, "Gee, that's kind of pretty, isn't it?" I looked at the little plastic manger scene on the floor under the tree, focusing on the little baby figure in the middle. "So, you're really who they say you are, huh?" I whispered.

It was getting late. I put the paperback down and got ready for bed. At that moment I honestly felt that what I had just done was somewhat intriguing, but probably would not amount to much in the long run. I can remember thinking it was an interesting way to pass the evening since I was out of beer.

When I went into my bedroom, there was no cake or candles or party hats visible in my house, but in the heavenly realm that evening, the celebration was nothing short of spectacular.

CHAPTER 13

IS THIS LOGICAL?

Shortly after having what I later realized was an authentic born again experience, I embarked on a methodical and determined quest to prove whether or not it really was true. The peace and serenity of that late-December night were quickly buried under an avalanche of doubts and questions.

I have always considered myself much more logical than emotional, and I felt a nagging suspicion that I may have been overcome by too much emotion when I prayed for Jesus to come into my life. I had to admit that I felt quite comforted by the whole thing and that the little bit of praying I had attempted since that night made me feel good. But I knew without a doubt that if it was just a little emotional trick I was playing on myself, it would never last. I had to prove to myself logically that it was true. Otherwise, the novelty would wear off and it would be just another dead-end attempt at happiness and fulfillment.

The question I kept asking myself was, "Do I believe this because it *is* true, or am I just saying I believe this because I *want* it to be true?" I didn't want to spend the rest of my life totally accepting a particular premise without having some proof. I felt that I had already made a similar mistake over the previous decade regarding the theory of evolution and all the secular, atheistic attitudes it produced. I had willingly accepted evolution without any analysis and based my entire world view on the notion that life appeared on this planet solely by random accident. I didn't want to take that same uneducated leap of faith with Jesus Christ. I had to find proof that this Christianity stuff was true.

As soon as I began studying the matter, it quickly became clear that everything about Christianity hinges on a couple of basic questions: Is Jesus who he said he is, and did he actually do what the Bible claims he did? If I could answer these two questions — was he really the son of God and did he really rise from the dead? — then I would be able to make an intelligent decision about my spiritual life. If he really was not who he claimed to be and if he really did not rise from the dead, then I did not want to waste any more time with it.

If he was just a well-spoken, charming philosopher whose teachings accidentally became the basis for a worldwide religion, I wasn't interested. I only wanted to be a part of it if he actually was alive now. I would remain interested only if I could actually bow my head in prayer and be in contact with him now. I didn't want to commit my life to a long-dead philosopher. I wanted a living, risen, son-of-the-almighty-creator savior. Yeah, I know it seems kind of demanding; I know I was acting like a Doubting Thomas. But that's just the way I am. If he was demanding my undivided devotion, then it only seemed

Is this Logical?

logical that I should demand that he really deserve it.

Before I could study the historical evidence for Jesus' deity and resurrection, I needed to journey down a few side roads. First of all, it quickly became obvious that the identity of Jesus Christ is a black and white, yes or no, issue. He was either the son of the living God, or he was a very defective person. There is no happy medium; there is no middle ground. Many people take the position that he was a good and wise human teacher, but not divine. But Jesus went to great lengths to make sure no one would draw that conclusion. He left only two choices as to his identity: the Lord of life and the savior of the world, or a crackpot.

Throughout his ministry, Jesus made a lot of startling claims about himself:[1]

* He considered himself to be morally perfect. "I have not come to destroy the Law but to fulfill it" (Matthew 5:17). "Your sins are forgiven" (Matthew 9:2).

* He seated all authority in himself. "All authority in heaven and on earth has been given to me" (Matthew 28:18).

* He spoke of the eternal world as though he had been there personally. "I saw Satan fall like lightning from heaven" (Luke 10:18). "Before Abraham was born, I am!" (John 8:58).

* He placed himself at the center of the religious universe. "I am the way, the truth and the life, no man comes to the Father except through me!" (John 14:6).

* He viewed his death as somehow necessary for the salvation of all mankind. "The Son of Man did not come to be served, but to serve, and to give his life as a ransom for many" (Mark 10:45).

* He claimed that he would be raised to life three days after his death. "The Son of Man will be betrayed...and

crucified. On the third day he will be raised to life" (Matthew 20:18-19).

Are these the statements of a good and wise human teacher? Of course not. If Jesus was a mere mortal and not divine, these claims make it clear that he was either quite deluded about his identity, or even worse, a cruel and calculating deceiver. He could only have been a liar, or a lunatic, or the Lord. There is no middle ground. He could not have been a good and wise human teacher.

Secondly, it became clear to me that there is no way anyone can "scientifically" prove that Jesus rose from the grave. By definition, proving a theory scientifically is accomplished by repeatedly observing an event under controlled conditions. When someone can predict that a particular event will happen, then create the conditions to make that event happen (or wait for the conditions to develop), and then carefully observe it happening numerous times as predicted, he is well on his way to proving the particular theory scientifically.

Since the whole point of Christianity is that a dead man got up and walked—but only once throughout all of history—it is obviously not possible to use scientific methods to prove or disprove it. No one can predict it will happen, create the conditions to make it happen, and then repeatedly observe it happening.

Like any study of an ancient event, I realized that I had to rely on the historical evidence. Scientific proof is not possible.

The final topic I needed to consider before looking into the details of Jesus' life and death was the biggest stumbling block of all: the whole question of natural versus supernatural. My atheistic, secular humanist background had trained me quite well to completely dismiss the notion that supernatural miracles could ever occur. I

Is this Logical?

was convinced that miraculous events (like virgin births, changing water into wine, resurrections, etc.) cannot possibly happen, therefore they have never happened, and therefore anyone claiming that they did happen is either a liar or a weak-minded looney tune.

I was like a person from the 16th century being told that it is possible for a man-made, metallic contraption to sail up into the air from one city and carry people safely to another city. If I had lived in the 16th century, I, of course, would have no knowledge of airplanes. The idea would simply fly (pardon the pun) in the face of everything I believed. So, before ever considering concepts such as aerodynamics or physics, I would have instantly dismissed the notion as sheer lunacy. Well, as a 20th century, science-based, modern man, I was inclined to approach religious faith and spirituality with a similar closed-minded bias.

It was, no doubt, a major obstacle. Often, people will say, "Well, in order to believe, what you must do is...believe." For me, this was about as helpful as telling a drowning man that all he has to do to keep from drowning is to start swimming. He already knows that!

I already knew that before I could move from the "I *want* this to be true" stage and into the "I know this *is* true" stage, I had to overcome my anti-supernatural bias.

For so long I was absolutely certain that nothing supernatural existed and the theory of evolution was, naturally and rationally, able to answer all the questions about life on earth. But when the glaring gaps in evolution's explanation of the origins of life became clear to me in that delivery room revelation, I knew there just had to be something which designed and then created life. I later realized that this something had to be what we call God.

Also — and this is the key idea — this creator God

must exist outside of nature. As the carpenter himself is not wood, and the artist himself is not made of paint and canvas, the creator of nature cannot be part of nature. Therefore, being outside of nature, God has to be, by definition, supernatural.

Hmm, supernatural.

This meant that God's designing and creating of natural life were most certainly supernatural acts. It finally dawned on me that the very existence of human life argues powerfully for the existence of a supernatural realm. It was out of this supernatural realm that our natural world was formed.

From this expanded point of view, I was finally able to accept that there must be a supernatural dimension somewhere out there. In fact, I now understood that our own births were miraculous events. If God could transform randomly swirling, inert molecules into complex, living, breathing, growing life forms, why couldn't he transform inert, dead flesh back into living tissue if he so chose? In other words, if he animated us once out of non-living material, why would it be impossible for him to re-animate one special person at one special time in history? My answer to this question, which frankly surprised me a lot considering my background, was that it was not impossible; if God wanted to do it, he was more than capable of doing it.

When my view of life reached this point, I still had doubts about whether the traditional stories of Christ's resurrection were accurate, but at least I had expanded from my nature-only frame of reference and acknowledged that it could have happened. Now I had to study all the historical evidence I could find and make an intelligent, logical decision about whether it did happen.

CHAPTER 14

WOW! THERE IS NO OTHER CONCLUSION

I knew the key to making an intelligent decision about the identity of Jesus Christ would hinge on the truth of the resurrection story. It is the central tenet of the Christian faith. It is what Jesus predicted he would do. It is what he pointed to as proof positive that he is who he claimed to be: God's one and only son and the savior of all mankind.

All the other aspects of Christianity are secondary: the virgin birth, the loaves and fishes, the healing of the blind and lame, the Golden Rule, the Sermon on the Mount, etc. If he did not rise up out of that tomb, then all these other things are nothing more than philosophical, feel-good fiction.

But if he did rise up out of that grave as he predicted, then everything else he said would carry much more weight. I think of it this way: if my next door neighbor comes over and tells me that he is the son of God and that he will be killed but then rise back to life three days later, I'm probably going to say, "Hey, Bob, maybe you'd better take a few sick days and get some rest, you're starting to make me nervous."

But if my next door neighbor dies and I go to the funeral and see him dead, and then three days later he's standing on my front porch with a big grin saying, "See, what did I tell you?" then I am going to listen a heck of a lot more closely to what he has to say. In fact, I'll probably go straight out and immediately organize the local branch of the First Church of Bob.

As mentioned in the last chapter, I knew I could not "scientifically" prove that Jesus rose from the dead. But if it were possible, I wanted to study the historical and circumstantial evidence, then attempt to determine why Jesus' followers began preaching that he rose from the grave. If I could find a logical, rational, non-supernatural explanation, then I was ready to conclude that Jesus did not actually rise and that the whole history of Christianity must be based on a misunderstanding or a hoax.

However, if I was unable to find a non-supernatural explanation after pouring over the available evidence, then I was ready to face the stunning conclusion that Jesus' followers were telling the truth.

Before listing the various theories of why the early apostles claimed the resurrection occurred, I should note some basic facts that even non-religious history scholars acknowledge to be true:[1]

(1) There was a man named Jesus who lived in Palestine at the beginning of what we now label the first century. If he was just a legend and never even lived, no sense spending time trying to decide if he rose from the dead.

(2) This man named Jesus got into trouble with the Jewish leaders in Jerusalem, was sentenced to death, and then crucified by the Roman authorities.

(3) Shortly after this, his followers went forth proclaiming a remarkable story which can be summarized as follows: After being executed, Jesus rose from his grave, appeared to them in bodily form quite alive and spoke with them and ate with them. Finally, his entire body rose up into the air and ascended to heaven.

(4) This story was the basis for the spread of the Christian religion, first in Palestine, and then throughout Asia and the Roman empire.

(5) The key to this Christian religion was belief in the actual, physical resurrection of Jesus. Without this belief, there was no religion.

(6) The Jewish leaders in Jerusalem were more motivated to disprove the preaching of Jesus' resurrection than anyone would be today. The Christian message undermined their religious authority and put added pressure on their already strained relationship with the Roman occupation army. In short, these Jewish leaders felt extremely threatened by the Jesus story and desperately wanted this new movement halted.

(7) The earliest disciples and apostles received terrible persecution for preaching this story about Jesus. Biblical and non-biblical historical records chronicle the brutal torture and deaths most of these people suffered because of the Jesus story.

(8) The documents which comprise our New Testament were written by eye-witnesses or their followers. Recent archaeological evidence shows that the original manuscripts for the New Testament were composed during the first century, much earlier than previously thought. The vast number of New Testament manuscripts

which have been discovered, over 24,000 to date (the Number Two document in all of history is Homer's *The Iliad,* with 643 surviving manuscripts),[2] shows that what the original authors wrote has been accurately passed down through the centuries. This does not mean the scholars believe that what was written is automatically true, but they are convinced that the original compositions have not been altered over the years.

Using these eight statements, which even non-religious scholars agree are true, as a foundation, I was ready to study the most prominent theories explaining why the resurrection story was preached by Jesus' disciples.[3]

The first two theories have been popular at various times in history, but upon close scrutiny, they both prove to be completely implausible.

* RESUSCITATION THEORY. This theory proposes that Jesus wasn't really dead. It was quite popular among 18th century rationalists. Jesus was merely unconscious on the cross and everyone thought he was dead. While in the cool of the tomb, he revived, appeared to his stunned followers, and the rest, as they say, is history. A variation on this theme was presented in the book, *The Passover Plot,* by Hugh Schoenfield, which claims that Jesus discovered a narcotic that could simulate death, tried it first on Lazarus, and then on himself as part of a brilliant scheme to deceive the world.

This theory ignores some pretty important facts, though. The Roman soldiers of that era are considered by military historians as possibly the most well-trained, highly-efficient, and brutally ruthless warriors of all time. Also, each soldier knew he could be immediately executed if he did not carry out his duty. It is inconceivable that any Roman soldier ordered to flog and crucify a prisoner could possibly have taken a still-breathing man down from the cross. In addition, Jesus' body was wrapped in grave clothes and up to 75 pounds of spices, gums, and resins. Even if he was alive, he would have suffocated from the burial preparations. As many people have noted, "This theory is more miraculous even than the resurrection itself."

* THE DISCIPLES WERE HALLUCINATING THEORY. This theory claims that the disciples thought they saw Jesus alive, but it was all in their heads; they were seeing things. This is highly unlikely for a couple of reasons. First, modern medicine teaches us that only particular kinds of people are prone to having hallucinations, usually paranoid or schizophrenic individuals. There is nothing in the historical records even remotely indicating the disciples were afflicted with these mental illnesses. Secondly, hallucinations are very personal occurrences. The chances that more than two people will have the same hallucination at the same time is virtually nil. With the early disciples, dozens and dozens of people claimed to have seen the risen Jesus at the same time.

The remainder of the theories attempting to explain the resurrection story in natural terms all boil down to one basic premise: the disciples were lying and they knew it.

* THE UNKNOWN TOMB THEORY. This theory states that most executed criminals of that era were dumped into a mass grave, therefore, no one could prove or disprove the disciples' story by pointing to the occupied tomb or producing Jesus' body. But since the disciples claimed they had seen Jesus alive, this theory means they were lying.

* THE DISCIPLES STOLE THE BODY THEORY. This would explain the empty tomb, but again, it means they were lying.

* JEWISH LEADERS OR ROMAN AUTHORITIES TOOK THE BODY THEORY. This theory explains the empty tomb, but it really makes no sense. Why would the authorities contribute to their own troubles? And why didn't they simply announce they took the body to counter the preaching of the disciples, or better yet, produce Jesus' rotting corpse? This would have silenced the disciples in an instant. Furthermore, even if this did happen, it doesn't explain the disciples' saying they saw Jesus alive, so they were still lying.

* THE WOMEN WENT TO THE WRONG TOMB THEORY. This theory states that those poor, confused, distraught women went to the wrong place in the cemetery. They saw an open tomb, got all excited, and the next thing you knew, a world-wide religion was off and running. This theory begs the question, Why didn't someone point out the *right* tomb? And if no one knew where the right tomb was, it still means the disciple's claims about seeing Jesus alive were lies.

* THE DISCIPLES MADE UP THE STORY TO SAVE FACE THEORY. This theory, frankly, makes the most sense and is the explanation I originally thought most probable. These people had invested three years of their lives following a dynamic leader and then suddenly it all went sour. Jesus got arrested and was executed and now all their dreams about being important people in his new kingdom were dashed. They made up the story so they could still be rich and famous.

These are the primary theories used to explain in natural terms how the resurrection story got started. Each theory, however, when boiled down to its most basic assumption, accuses the disciples of knowingly promoting fraudulent claims. Now let me explain how I came to believe that these people were not lying, could not have been lying, and that the correct theory about the resurrection is:

* THE DISCIPLES WERE HONESTLY REPORTING WHAT THEY SAW AND EXPERIENCED THEORY.

The key to believing that the disciples were being honest is summed up in one sentence: Nobody dies for a lie, especially alone. If a supernatural event did not occur — if Jesus did not rise from the grave — then these people invented this resurrection story and conspired to promote it. A basic understanding of human nature tells us that people will enter into conspiracies and promote lies only when they're getting something out of it (think of businessmen and politicians for some obvious examples).

If the early disciples were receiving fame and fortune, power and prestige because of the resurrection story, then I would be inclined to think they were liars and chalk it up to human nature. But when the conspiracy and the lying bring nothing but trouble, much more trouble than telling the truth could ever bring, then basic human nature suggests that people will come clean in a New York minute and distance themselves from the conspiracy.

The early disciples of Jesus, the people who came forth claiming to have seen Jesus' bodily resurrection and ascension into heaven, were all persecuted terribly because of the story. In fact, all but one, the apostle John, ended up being executed as a result. Most importantly, there is not one shred of evidence in any historical record indicating that any of these people ever recanted the story to save their hides. They suffered and died with this story still on their lips.

I am convinced that human beings who enter into a conspiracy with the idea of gaining something will not stick to the bogus story when it means torture and death. I found the list of people who died because of their claims about Jesus to be stunning:[4]

James, son of Zebedee - preached the Jesus story in Judea. Killed with a sword by King Herod Antipas.

Thomas - preached the Jesus story in India. Killed with a Brahman sword near Madras.

Bartholomew - preached the Jesus story in Armenia. Skinned alive with a whip and died.

Mark - preached the Jesus story in Egypt. Burned to death at Bucolus.

Andrew - preached the Jesus story in Ethiopia. Crucified on an X-shaped cross.

Philip - preached the Jesus story in Phrygia. Crucified at Hierapolis.

James, relative of Jesus - preached the Jesus story in Judea. Stoned to death.

Simon the Zealot - preached the Jesus story in Mauritania and Africa. Crucified.

Matthew - preached the Jesus story in Ethiopia and Egypt. Killed with a spear by King Hircanus.

Jude - preached the Jesus story in Assyria and Persia. Killed in Persia.

Peter - preached the Jesus story in Judea and Rome. Crucified upside down in Rome.

Paul, apostle to the Gentiles who claimed to have been personally instructed by Jesus some years after the resurrection - preached the Jesus story throughout Asia and the Roman empire. Beheaded in Rome by Emperor Nero.

Liars and conspirators would not have allowed these things to happen to themselves.

The real clincher for me is that all these people suffered and died *alone*. I can maybe see someone sticking to a conspiracy unto death if his other co-conspirators are right there with him. Maybe the peer pressure not to be the first one to squeal will make a person hold fast to the fraudulent story — maybe. But all these disciples were far away from their fellow conspirators when they suffered. And this was during an age long before phones, faxes, e-mail, Action News Mobile Cam, and 24-hour satellite news networks. If any of them in those remote locations had recanted the Jesus story to keep from dying, none of their pals would have ever found out. It is absolutely impossible to think these people made up a lie and then suffered and died alone for it.

When I reached this point in my study of the resurrection, I shook my head and slowly whispered, "Wow, they really were telling the truth. Jesus must have risen from that tomb."

CHAPTER 15

MORE EVIDENCE - A CHANGED LIFE

To summarize the last few chapters:

I came to believe that there exists an all-powerful, all-knowing, creator God. This God exists in a supernatural realm and He created our natural world and us in it. The existence of this supernatural realm means it is not impossible for a supernatural event to occur in our natural world, if God so chooses.

After studying all the theories which attempt to explain how the Christian religion could have been formed if Jesus did not rise from the grave, I realized that none adequately explain how it happened, and the early apostles must have been telling the truth. I finally accepted, to my complete surprise, the idea that Jesus did indeed rise from the tomb, giving authority to everything else he said about himself. Therefore, his claims of being the son of God, the savior of the world, and our one true path to eternal salvation, also should be believed.

Now, what I've done in these past few chapters is describe my search for reasonable and logical proof that the resurrection of Christ really did occur. My time-consuming research, however, does not in any way demonstrate that I am such a loyal and faithful disciple. On the contrary, it really shows just how skeptical and wimpy my faith can be.

The Bible clearly teaches that "faith is being sure of what we hope for and certain of what we do not see" (Hebrews 11:1). And again, "We live by faith, not by sight" (2 Corinthians 5:7). When you boil it all down, true faith in Christ ultimately is not the result of page after page of logical analysis, it is the result of opening your heart and letting his glorious spirit dwell within you.

I spent a lot of time pouring over the evidence and the numerous analyses which demonstrate that the claims of the Bible can be accepted as true, reasonably and logically. But my desire to spend so much time investigating this was due mostly to my doubts and uncertainties.

Even after it became obvious intellectually that I could trust that the Gospel message was true, my 20th century, skeptical, secular humanist background made it very difficult for me to embrace it wholeheartedly. In my head I was able tentatively to acknowledge that the lessons of my long ago Sunday School classes were accurate, in a detached and distant sort of way. But it wasn't until I accepted the truth about Jesus in my heart — by faith and not by sight — that his supernatural power became plainly evident.

The final and convincing proof that Jesus is who he claimed to be did not come from a stack of dry and detailed analytical documents, but rather from the miraculous transformation of a self-centered, irresponsible, chronic alcoholic into a thankful, grateful, and humble (occasionally) family man. In other words, I changed from a flaming jerk into a real human being. And I am convinced that it could not have happened without the help of a supernatural, spiritual power which I did not in any way possess beforehand.

Soon after my born again experience on that late December evening, a major change occurred between me and my closest friend: alcohol. It wasn't that I suddenly stopped drinking and now believed that getting drunk was wrong. I just didn't enjoy it anymore. Something was missing. That burning desire to be intoxicated and to escape reality had disappeared. Each time I drank, I waited for that overwhelming relief, that comfortable "Ahhhhh..." feeling to envelop me as drunkenness set in. But it was gone. I did not become comfortably numb anymore. Instead, a quite remarkable and thoroughly unexpected feeling came over me: I would rather be sober!

It was as if everything in the world was turned upside down. Black was white and white was black. Sobriety, the state of being undrunk, was now the more comfortable state of mind. Pouring a six-pack of Budweiser down my gullet now made me UN-comfortable. Frankly, I was shocked. From the time I sipped that first beer in high school I had carefully surrounded myself with like-minded friends and associates. And our like-minded view was right to the point: drinking is great; being drunk makes us happy.

Now, something had changed within me. I was finding happiness from a different source. I liked being alert and clear-headed; it was a new and exciting feeling. My alcoholic consumption was slashed to almost zero. It wasn't until years later that I understood it was the power of

Jesus' spirit dwelling in me which caused the change. At that time, however, I did not make the connection.

It was a strange sensation, to say the least. On the one hand, I enjoyed being refreshed and alive in the morning instead of being hung over. I found myself with lots of free time and energy to do useful things around the house and at my office. And I was saving a lot of money that used to disappear in liquor stores and taverns. (My favorite bar went out of business a few months later. I am assuming, of course, that it was just a coincidence. I mean, really, one man — even a big-time juicer — can't single-handedly keep a saloon in business, can he?)

During this entire period, however, I was more than a little confused. Drinking had always been my most cherished activity. All my close friends were heavy drinkers. Now, a major part of my life, admittedly a very destructive part, was gone. There was a big void. Despite all the positive changes at home and work, I was feeling a sense of loss. Finally, one evening as I was sitting in my office thinking about drinking, but knowing that I wouldn't find any pleasure in it anymore, a remarkable event occurred. Without giving it any thought, I suddenly grabbed the phone book, looked up the number for Alcoholics Anonymous, and dialed. I can only attribute this to the power of the Holy Spirit, since at the time I had no idea what the organization was all about and even less of an idea why I was calling them. As the phone was ringing I had a frantic conversation with myself.

"Why did I dial this number?". . ."I don't know."

"What am I going to say when they answer?". . ."I have no idea."

"What's going on here, anyway?!". . ."Beats the heck out of me, pal."

When the phone was finally answered, I blurted out,

More Evidence - A Changed Life

"I, uh...I want to talk to someone about drinking."

"Well, you've come to the right place, my friend," was the calm and reassuring reply.

Eventually, it was arranged for me to attend an A.A. meeting, and a whole new world was opened up. Never before had I been among a group of people so humble, so caring, and so hopeful. They were the exact opposite of the cynical, bitter, false-bravado crowd with whom I had associated for so long at the bars. Ironically, just about all of them had at one time been a part of that hopeless, bitter, escape-from-reality multitude. But they had come out of the darkness and entered into the light. Now I was in the process of doing the same.

Later on, I was able to understand much more clearly what was actually happening at this point in time. Jesus Christ had instantaneously removed my physical and emotional dependence on alcohol. Then he led me to a group of people who could fill the huge void in my life which had been caused by the sudden absence of drinking and drinking-related activities. Additionally, this group of people helped me catch up on the emotional development which had been stunted since high school. (Remember, as I mentioned in a previous chapter, the alcohol addiction had caused me to be a 27-year-old man with the emotional maturity of a 16-year-old.)

This became the additional proof that clinched it in my mind. All that historical research and all that analysis and all that logical studying was fine; it all indicated that Jesus is who he claimed to be. But now I had living proof, I *was* living proof. He had done the impossible. He had converted me. And not so much a conversion from a secular person into a religious person, but more of a conversion from a despairing and lost soul into a saved and hopeful soul.

He is definitely who he claimed to be back when he walked the earth 2,000 years ago. And he is definitely alive right now and just waiting to come into the life of anyone who will only ask him by faith. And I must point out that this has nothing to do with "religion" per se. It does, however, have everything to do with entering into a proper relationship with that awesome Being who created us. Churches and creeds and liturgies and charities and hymns and potluck suppers and wearing your Easter bonnet with all the frills upon it are fine and dandy. But it is all meaningless if you don't understand who God is and what his son Jesus did for us. When you put your faith in these undeniable truths, then everything else falls into place.

I once heard a fellow recovering drunk explain how Jesus had changed his life. In an ungrammatical, inarticulate way, it was one of the most eloquent things I have ever heard. It went something like this: "Some people say that Jesus can do miracles. They say he once changed water into wine. Well, I don't know nothin' about that, it wasn't like I was there, y'know. But I do know that he changed wine into bread...and into furniture...and into rent money...and into love. He changed a bum into a man. He changed a loser into a daddy. And that's a pretty fine miracle if you ask me."

CHAPTER 16

TIME - A DIFFERENT PERSPECTIVE

One of the more interesting aspects of becoming a believer in God was the drastic change in the way I perceived time. Up until my conversion, I was a practitioner of what I like to call "dog thinking." With dog thinking, the past is meaningless, the future is incomprehensible, and all time consists of nothing more than a steady stream of moments called "now." In other words, I lived entirely for the present.

This is exactly the way every dog — well, at least my Phi Beta Kappa of a dog — perceives time. No matter how often I come home from work at precisely 5:30 p.m. each and every day, my dog is totally shocked when I walk through that door. And she demonstrates her surprise and amazement by barking wildly, running around in circles, and finally peeing on the floor. Every day it's as if she has been stranded alone on a desert island and I'm the Coast Guard rescue boat pulling up on shore. She is utterly thunderstruck by this turn of events. You would think the fact that this identical scenario has occurred now over 3,000 times in her 14-year lifetime would somehow sink into her tiny little brain. But she's a dog, and dog brains apparently are not capable of grasping the concept of "the past."

We humans, on the other hand, can't use this excuse. Our brains are capable of studying the past, learning from it, and applying it to our lives. But many of us, especially the baby boom generation, have not bothered to avail ourselves of this intellectual ability. This is obvious in many of the popular baby boomer slogans: "If it feels good, do it!" "If you can't be with the one you love, love the one you're with." "Do your own thing." "Don't trust anyone over 30!"

None of these mottos demonstrate much understanding of the past (not to mention a shred of common sense). Nor do they demonstrate that any thought has been given to the future. Baby boomers are notorious for their lack of planning. For example, any generation which has so little chance of ever seeing a nickel from the Social Security and Medicare programs and still only saves about three cents out of every thousand dollars earned, is not showing much of a grasp of the concept of "later."

All the years before I came to know the Lord, it was as if I was traveling along a time trail through an overgrown jungle. Chronologically speaking, I was unable to see either two feet in front of me or two feet behind me. It was a day to day trudge along the path of time, and I was not very sure of where I had come from and even less aware of where I was going.

After becoming a Christian, however, I was seemingly elevated far above the jungle and now could look back down the time trail and see where I had been. Also, I could gaze forward and feel much more sure about what the future would bring.

I suddenly felt connected with the past. My life was no longer a random, isolated, cosmic accident (as the Darwinists claim), but rather it was part of a specific plan God himself had designed for the human race.

My 11th grade history teacher would be stunned to learn that my interest in studying history has now blossomed. Back in his class, my concern for past events was limited to thinking about what I had eaten for lunch an hour earlier. Anything at all more distant past than that was an absolute bore.

But now I began to realize that the events of the past have a great influence on present-day circumstances. And more importantly, I began to understand that the ideas of the past could be very useful to us here in the present. I was able to shed, as C.S. Lewis defined it, the "chronological snobbery" which afflicts far too many people. This is the notion that all current ideas are automatically better and more truthful than any past ideas simply because they are *our* ideas.[1] We tend to think that since past generations were not capable of flying to the moon or splitting the atom, then they were also not capable of truly understanding such topics as human nature, social dynamics, and philosophy.

A study of historic human wisdom, especially Biblical wisdom, shows that it is our present generation which is truly ignorant when it comes to these topics. Chronological snobbery compels us to dismiss a particular idea just because it has gone out of style, rather than because it has been logically and systematically discredited. So many of the views which govern our culture today are accepted simply because they are new, not because they have any track record of being true.

I was surprised to discover that documents written two- to three-thousand years ago display a far better understanding of human nature than much of the pop-psychology currently in vogue today. (Of course, when you also believe that these documents were inspired by God himself, the creator of humans and human nature, you are not that surprised after all.)

So, despite all our marvelous discoveries during the past century in the technological realm, we have rapidly regressed during the same time period toward a barbarian level in the cultural realm.

Although being able to look back clearly down the time trail of the past gave me a new understanding of myself and the world, the view forward is infinitely more exciting. Christianity, in a nutshell, opens up an eternal perspective on the future. Instead of my life being a century-or-less minuscule blip on the cosmic time line, I now see that it is only my physical, natural life that is brief and finite. My soul and my mind, the true essence of my being, will exist for eternity. Way cool, as they say.

From this perspective, when you take the natural 60, 80-, or 100-year life span and then add to it a few gazillion centuries (which is really only adding a fraction of the first *day* of eternity to it), the view of our natural life changes drastically. On the one hand, values and priorities shift. The things that people take so seriously are now seen for what they are: fleeting, momentary, and not such a big deal after all. Christians generally view life with much less angst and panic, no longer distraught to see it quickly passing by. In an ironic twist, when we release our frantic grip on temporal matters, we actually enjoy them more.

On the other hand, this new eternal perspective makes us appreciate much more what a gift this natural

Time - A Different Perspective

life is. Of all the people who have ever lived in the past or will ever live in the future, only we few (five billion a few? Well, yes, relatively speaking) have the privilege of being alive today. Realizing the magnitude of this gift, we feel a greater urge to make the most of it. Who wants to spend all of eternity lamenting about how this one, special opportunity was squandered?

The best way I can describe the Christian view of time and life is with an analogy: Imagine a man is required to take a 100 mile journey and is given two travel options. With the first choice, he will ride to his destination in a stretch limo with a fully-stocked bar, buffet table, and a satellite TV. With the second option, he must ride to his destination on a bicycle with a bottle of water and a baloney sandwich. Now, if this is all there is to the situation, then most people will choose the first, seemingly more enjoyable, option.

But suppose the 100 mile journey is only the beginning. Suppose the man is required to spend the next twenty years living in this new destination. And further, suppose that the circumstances of the next twenty years will be based solely on which travel option he selects. If he chooses to ride in the limo, he will spend the next twenty years living in a run-down shack and working at a tedious, back-breaking job. But if he chooses to travel on the bicycle, he will spend the next twenty years living in a magnificent palace, and working — or not working, if that's his preference — at whatever occupation he wants.

This certainly changes the equation and should cause most people to alter their selection. Instead of a couple hours in a lavish limo, they will choose to put up with the long bike ride because of the much more valuable reward waiting at the end of the journey.

This is how Christians view life. We know that our

long-term situation is based on how we choose to travel through this life. We also realize that this journey of life is quite brief compared to our eternal destination, and so we choose to forego the easy but fleeting pleasure and instead opt for the arduous but much more rewarding path.

To top it all off, imagine that in my little scenario, the ride in the stretch limo turns out to be a disaster: the air conditioning doesn't work; the shocks are broken so the ride is bumpy; the bar has nothing but cheap gin which makes you queasy; the food on the buffet is spoiled; and the satellite TV picks up nothing but the two-hour version of the Flo-Bee info-mercial. It's not at all as enjoyable as you thought.

While at the same time the bike ride surprisingly turns out to be a delight: the weather is wonderful, the scenery spectacular, the road smooth and flat, and you meet many friendly people along the way who share their food, drink, and companionship with you.

Again, this is similar to the Christian life. What was at first thought to be somber and dreary — the decision to follow Jesus and forsake hedonistic living — turns out to be far more joyful and fulfilling. There's a lot to be said for a life free from bill collectors, communicable diseases, disgruntled ex-wives, arrest warrant-toting detectives, and D.W.I. counseling sessions; not to mention knowing that you're living your life in accordance (as best you can) with God's wishes. Talk about liberation!

CHAPTER 17

POLITICS

I was never very interested in politics when I was growing up. For one thing, it's chock full of politicians. That fact alone is enough to turn off most people. But the opinions I did hold were generally left-leaning and had been shaped by three sources:

1. My family. I come from a long line of FDR-loving, urban, Northeastern, Democratic Party loyalists. My family tree is loaded with union members, civil servants, and military careerists. I'm certain the word "wealthy" has never been used to describe any of my relatives. If a Dunn, Healy, Casey, or Cavanaugh was ever spotted at a fancy country club, it was because he was either bussing tables or carrying some Republican's golf bag. To us, Jimmy Stewart as good-hearted George Bailey represented the ideal Democrat, and Lionel Barrymore as mean old Mr. Potter was the typical greedy Republican.

2. My openly socialist professors in college. They

constantly preached that the rich always get rich at the expense of the poor, all wealth should be immediately redistributed, a one-world government should rule the planet, and the ubiquitous concept of "fairness" (of outcome, not of opportunity or rights) should dominate all thoughts, deeds, and public policies.

3. My personal secular humanist philosophy. Believing that the concept of "God" was a silly, ancient superstition, I naturally dismissed the idea that a divine moral law governs all human endeavors. I was convinced that there is no such thing as absolute truth and that the definition of right and wrong should be left to each individual. The worst crime anyone could ever commit would be to "impose" his values on someone else. As we shall see a bit later, this notion is the fatal flaw of modern liberalism.

There is a quotation generally attributed to Winston Churchill: "If a man is not liberal at age 20 he has no heart, and if he is not conservative at age 40 he has no brain."[1]

Despite being more of a wise-crack than a profundity, this quote pretty well sums up how my views have been transformed. I'm sure part of my shift from liberalism to conservatism was due to the natural aging and maturing process: starting a family, buying a house, and paying taxes. But becoming a Christian really opened my eyes to the basic errors of liberal political thought. If I had remained a secular humanist, I'm not sure whether I would have stayed loyal to the ideology of the left. If I was still a pagan, I suppose it's possible I could be worshipping today at the altar of Bill and Hillary's Big Government Nanny State, but I sincerely hope not.

However, when I became a Christian (and long before I ever heard of Rush or Newt, by the way) my understanding of the nature and source of truth and values completely changed.

To better understand, a brief history lesson is in order. For thousands of years, civilized societies understood that a moral law, a code of ethics, governed human relations. The Judeo-Christian heritage believed this moral law came from God himself, the supernatural creator of both the world and mankind.

But even non-Judeo-Christian cultures understood that a firm, moral code existed. The Greek philosopher Aristotle, certainly not a Jew or a Christian, taught that there is an ethical law based on universal human nature. This came to be known as the Natural Law.[2]

The key is that this firm, ethical code did not come from any individual or group. It originated outside of man, either from God or from Nature. Most people understood that the basic principles of the moral law were not open for debate since they were based on human nature and no matter how much someone objected, human nature was not about to change.

These laws were not very complicated. It's basic stuff: Killing or injuring an innocent person is wrong; stealing or damaging his property is wrong; honesty is better than lying; hard work is better than laziness; self-control is better than lust; sacrificing for your children is better than being self-indulgent.

For thousands of years societies understood that if citizens strove to meet these universal ideals (acknowledging, of course, that people will often fall short), then the civilization had the best chance of thriving and each individual had the best chance of living a satisfied, fulfilled life.

But in the 17th century, a whole new way of viewing life emerged. This new philosophy, often referred to as

The Enlightenment or the Age of Reason, rejected the concept of a firm, universal moral law. Morals and ethics did not come from God or Nature, it was argued, but instead came from within each person. The individual should define right and wrong for himself based on his own feelings and desires.

Moral and ethical authority suddenly shifted from outside of the individual to solely within each individual. There was no longer any absolute standard of right and wrong. Truth was now relative. One man's definition of right and wrong now could be the complete opposite of another man's.

This humanist philosophy, I sincerely believe, is dead wrong. It plays right into the hands of mankind's prideful, selfish ego. No doubt, it's a real ego boost to claim sole authority for the definition of truth, but it's far too familiar to the all-time original lie, when Satan convinced Adam and Eve to turn away from God by promising, "You will be like God" (Genesis 3:5).

People generally don't need much encouragement to get caught up in worshipping themselves. The Enlightenment thinking suddenly made this narcissistic attitude fashionable. It is, without a doubt, the root cause of both the present-day cultural decay and the overwhelming flood of individual unhappiness we see everywhere.

Another product of the Enlightenment philosophy was the concept than people are basically good and only social structures are evil. Moral effort was shifted away from personal ethics and towards politics and economics. To paraphrase Charles Colson in his marvelous book, *A Dance With Deception*, this view rejected the biblical doctrine of sin and mankind's innate depravity, and saw no need for a society to have strong moral restraints to keep sin from bursting forth and undermining the social order.³

Ironically, the idea of mankind's "original sin" is one of the few philosophical theories which has been empirically proven beyond a doubt. Thousands and thousands of years of recorded human history conclusively demonstrate that when left to his own unrestrained instincts, man's two most prominent traits are selfishness and cruelty.

Following this misguided view, people assume that a society should be able to grow and improve by directing its resources toward social structures alone. Individual moral character is not important. We see evidence of this thinking nowadays. All of our problems, we are told, come from poverty, racism, sexism, homophobia, unequal distribution of wealth, a lack of gun control, intolerant patriarchal churches, strict disciplinarian families, etc.

If anyone even attempts to suggest that individual responsibility and personal character may also be important, he is immediately shouted down as an ignorant boob trying to "impose" his values on someone else. (Or take your pick of other popular epithets: extremist, religious nut, radical, right-winger, intolerant, fundamentalist, greedy, Religious Reich, mean-spirited, etc.)

But many decades (and many trillions of dollars) of trying to improve society with liberal solutions have resulted in conditions becoming dramatically worse. The liberal analysis of this whole situation: we haven't spent enough money. The conservative analysis: handing out cash without any personal responsibility required is like trying to cure lung cancer with more cigarettes.

No matter how sincere our efforts, no matter how compassionate we claim to be, no matter how much money we spend, liberal solutions to social problems can never be successful. The fundamental misunderstanding of human nature which is at the heart of liberalism — that evil comes solely from external sources rather than from within individual human hearts — has doomed it to certain failure.

For example, how often are we told nowadays that the root cause of a particular anti-social or criminal act is really our unjust, oppressive society? It's not polite to suggest that the individual simply made a conscious decision to do something wrong. The person who committed the crime was *deprived,* not *depraved,* liberal apologists tell us.

This ridiculous point of view offends normal sensibilities for two reasons. First, this is a direct insult and a slap in the face to every decent, law-abiding person who came from a disadvantaged background. Secondly, this attitude portrays the real criminals as the "victims" and the real victims as the "criminals." There is no surer formula for anarchy. Taking this liberal lunacy to its logical conclusion, every person who has ever experienced the plight of being poor, or a racial/ethnic minority, or the offspring of a single parent, or a sexually-harassed woman, or, who knows, maybe even the recipient of improper toilet training, should go out and get an Uzi and shoot up a shopping mall. And then, I suppose, the law-abiding segment of society (at least the ones still standing) should thank this unfortunate "victim" for having the courage to express his frustration toward the oppressive cultural forces which so very unfairly denied him his right to a perfectly blissful and happy life. (See, you can have a lot of wacky fun when you get past the bleeding heart platitudes and really start analyzing the eventual outcome of liberal ideology.)

It all originates with a basic misunderstanding of human nature. When you believe evil comes from immoral social systems rather than from individuals making immoral personal decisions, then all your efforts will be focused on social engineering programs. And when the social engineering programs exacerbate the problem, you are unable to admit it because your philosophical framework does not allow for that possibility.

But if you correctly understand human nature and know that personal character must be addressed first before attempting to rectify any social systems, then you have a fighting chance of improving conditions, or at the very least, of staving off the disintegration of civilization.

Another related topic which demonstrates the liberal misunderstanding of human nature is economics. According to liberals, the people in a society who work hard and produce wealth should transfer a significant portion of their assets (in the name of "fairness") to the segment of society which does not work and produce wealth. Liberals actually think that when the government imposes this system onto an economy, the behaviors of both groups will remain unchanged. But in reality, when achievers are penalized for achieving, they'll cease to be industrious. And when non-achievers are rewarded for their sloth, the hope that they will one day become industrious disappears.

Any economic system which punishes responsible behavior (discipline, achievement, and success) and subsidizes irresponsible behavior (instant gratification, illegitimacy, and laziness) is bound to cause more problems than it solves. It's just a matter of time before every segment of society falls far short of its potential — economic and otherwise — since all incentives to work hard and prosper have been removed.

And from the Christian point of view, it is this falling so far short of potential which is most tragic. Sure, we'd like a safer, more orderly society. Sure, we'd like to have less of our hard-earned money confiscated by the tax man. But Christians honestly believe that every single person has been created by God, in His image, with a precious opportunity to make the most of his or her life. To see our own government follow a philosophy which panders to the lowest common denominator of human nature, and then virtually enslave a large chunk of the population in a hopeless system of wasted human potential, is the real tragedy.

Now, this doesn't mean that I'm a big fan of cut-throat, cold-hearted, profit-obsessed, greed-driven capitalism. (Of course, when you compare capitalism with socialism, it's a no-brainer. Socialism seems to be based on the idea that since everybody can't be prosperous, let's set up a system which guarantees that nobody will be prosperous.) However, unlike many of my enthusiastic free-market friends who insist that ethics and morality have nothing to do with "the business of business," I am convinced that any economic system which is devoid of a moral component is doomed to fail. As I've always said (ever since I thought it up a few minutes ago), "Pagan capitalism is little better than pagan socialism: whether you seek fulfillment by desperately filling your closet with shoes or desperately searching for food, you're still desperate."

Sure, everyone on all sides of the political spectrum is in favor of a strong and thriving economy. It's the best way to improve the lot of as many people as possible. But to cite Charles Colson again: "What are the factors that make for a thriving economy? Well, for starters, people have to be willing to work hard; that's motivation and self-sacrifice. They have to be willing to honor contracts; that's honesty and fidelity. They have to invest time and effort in projects that pay off only in the future; that's self-discipline and delayed gratification. People have to cooperate with co-workers; that's kindness and respect. Lawmakers have to pass bills for industry that are fair and consistent; that's integrity.

"The conclusion is obvious. The marketplace depends on people holding high ethical standards. Values aren't peripheral to the economy....Values are the very *heart* of the economy."[4]

Those free-market libertarians who insist that unfettered capitalism will solve all our problems are as deluded as the utopian Marxists. When the moral dimension of any human activity is ignored, trouble is sure to follow.

So, to summarize, my politics are an extension of my philosophy (which is an extension of my religion). And my philosophy tells me that a transcendent, absolute, moral law governs all human endeavors. This moral code of ethics exists (I believe it came from God) because no civilization can long survive if its citizens are given the license to indulge their every whim and craving. Any culture which focuses on rampant individualism and totally ignores the common good will surely have a bleak future. In other words, a culture will collapse if it embraces such juvenile concepts as "If it feels good, do it!" or "If you can't be with the one you love, love the one you're with!" or "Do your own thing!" (Ringing any bells here, baby boomers?)

The words of George Washington, upon becoming our first president in 1789, say it best, "The propitious smiles of Heaven can never be expected on a nation that disregards the eternal rules of order and right which Heaven itself has ordained."[5]

My politics are conservative for one simple reason: I have grown fond of this country, the land my children and grandchildren will one day inherit, and I truly believe no nation can survive a series of Me Generations.

CHAPTER 18

NOT AFRAID OF DEATH

Have you ever been to a funeral where there were a lot of agnostics and skeptics in attendance? Have you noticed how they simply refuse to look directly at the guest of honor? That dead body lying there in the middle of the room is just too disturbing. It reminds them of the one thing they've tried so hard to put out of their minds: the fact that we all will die someday.

If you are convinced that our natural, physical life is all there is, if you truly believe that upon death we cease to exist, then attending funerals or contemplating mortality can be downright torturous.

How different it is with many Christians. In some churches they are so sure that the deceased's soul has gone on to a glorious heavenly reward, they don't bother having funeral services. They have graduation ceremonies. Talk about chutzpah. It takes a lot of faith and courage to look death straight in the eye and laugh.

But that's exactly what faith in Jesus can do. The whole point of Christianity, the whole Gospel message, is that Christ has conquered death and we can, too. If it's not true, then everything else is a waste of time. The apostle Paul says as much in his first letter to the Corinthians: "For if the dead are not raised, then Christ has not been raised either. And if Christ has not been raised, your faith is futile...If only for this life we have hope in Christ, we are to be pitied more than all men" (1 Corinthians 15:16-19).

There are a lot of earthly benefits to being a Christian: emotional peace, serenity, sobriety, etc. But if there is no hope for eternal life, if the secular humanists are correct that life is a random, meaningless accident which ends tragically at the moment of death, then we might as well crack open a bottle of tequila and max out the VISA and MasterCard right now.

The hope and faith in eternal life is the key difference between Christians and secular humanists. Contrast those believers who have joyful graduation ceremonies for their deceased loved ones with the pain and hopelessness of atheists.

Bertrand Russell was a famous scholar, author, and outspoken atheist. After he died, his daughter, Katherine Tait, said of the despair that gripped him, "Somewhere at the bottom of his heart, in the depths of his soul, there was an empty space that once had been filled by God, and he never found anything else to put in it."[1]

Russell not only had some miserable times, apparently, during his life, but if his soul is eternal, as I believe and as the Bible teaches, then right at this moment and forevermore, he's *really* miserable.

Another famous atheist, playwright George Bernard Shaw, wrote these chilling words shortly before he died in 1950: "The science to which I pinned my faith is bankrupt. Its counsels, which should have established the millennium, have led directly to the suicide of Europe. I believed them once. In their name I helped to destroy the faith of millions. And now they look at me and witness the great tragedy of an atheist who has lost his faith."[2]

An atheist who has lost his faith. Wow. He rejected God and then he rejected the rejection of God. A man truly lost and without hope.

And that is one of the most prominent features of our modern, secular world: a lack of hope. Never has a society in all the world's history been at the same time so abundantly blessed with material goods and so devoid of spiritual serenity. Despite the high percentage of citizens claiming to be church-going believers, the secular influences of our culture, with an emphasis on doubt and skepticism, have reduced a once clear and confident hope into a vague and tentative wish. "I *wish* there was something to believe in, but how can I know for sure?" seems to be the general attitude these days.

So we continue to accumulate the fancy toys and seek fulfillment and meaning in all the wrong places. And the more we achieve power and prestige according to the world's standards, the more empty we feel inside. It's like adding a second floor to a house with no foundation. It may look good for a while, but eventually it will collapse into a heap.

But the Good News of the Gospel is that we *can* have hope. If we trust in Him who designed the heavens and laid out the foundations of the earth, if we believe in the eternal God of the Universe, we can be filled with hope—and joy and peace.

Jesus himself said, "Do not let your hearts be troubled. Trust in God; trust also in me. In my Father's house are many rooms; if it were not so, I would have told you. I am going there to prepare a place for you. And if I go and prepare a place for you, I will come back and take you to be with me that you also may be where I am" (John 14:1-3).

The letter to the Hebrews states: "...by his death Jesus...destroyed him who holds the power of death — that is, the devil — and freed those who all their lives were held in slavery by their fear of death" (Hebrews 2:14-15).

Anyone enslaved by a fear of death need only trust in the saving power of Christ. As the Bible verse made famous on countless end zone placards says: "For God so loved the world that he gave his one and only Son, that whoever believes in him shall not perish but have eternal life" (John 3:16).

This assurance, this hope, this confidence in eternal life makes all the difference. It is what allows us to live as "James Bond Christians."

Well, OK, I'd better explain that one:

When I was a kid, I just loved those James Bond movies (and Sean Connery had it all over Roger Moore, by the way, no contest). The greatest thing about the character, Agent 007, was that no matter how perilous the situation became, he was always as cool as a cucumber. It was as if he *knew* no harm could ever come to him.

I can remember being about 10 years old and discussing this with my friends. "How come he never gets scared? It's like he knows the bad guys can't get him."

"Ya bonehead! Of course the bad guys can't get him. He's James Bond! He's the hero. Everybody knows he's gonna win! Ian Fleming wrote the books that way."

"Yeah, but, while it's happening, he's not 'spose to know he's part of the story. Technically, James Bond's not 'spose to know Ian Fleming wrote it out like that. I mean, he should be scared a little bit, right?"

"Ah, ya bonehead! He's James Bond! He just *knows*, all right?!"

I can remember thinking that it would be so great to *know* that my life was part of a grand script — with me as the hero — and that no matter how awful a situation might be, everything would ultimately turn out fine. Then I could relax and not be scared and maybe be almost as cool as James Bond. (Of course, when I winked at my 5th grade teacher and said, "Hello, beautiful. I'll have a vodka martini with a twist...shaken, not stirred," that particular situation didn't turn out so fine.)

Well, despite being a weird analogy, this is what the Christian faith allows us to do. God has assured us that we are part of his grand plan in which we shall be, unequivocally and absolutely, victorious. When an eternal perspective is added to our natural life-span, we are able to realize that no matter what happens here and now, our ultimate fate is victory and glory.

Paul explained it in his letter to the Romans: "For I am convinced that neither death nor life, neither angels nor demons, neither the present nor the future, nor any powers, neither height nor depth, nor anything else in all creation, will be able to separate us from the love of God that is in Christ Jesus our Lord" (Romans 8:38-39).

With a faith and a hope such as this, we can handle whatever comes our way just like "James Bond Christians." We simply know that the bad guys can't get us. Even if it's joblessness, or homelessness, or cancer, or a head-on collision which ends our life instantly, we simply know that God has prepared in advance a marvelous place for us.

As Paul wrote to the Philippians: "To me, to live is Christ and to die is gain....Yet what shall I choose? I do not know! I am torn between the two: I desire to depart and be with Christ, which is better by far" (Philippians 1:21-23).

Now, I'm sure this whole discussion evokes in some people the exact same feelings I had long before I became a believer. You wacko religious nuts, I used to think, you're so caught up in this life-after-death fantasy of heaven, that you forget to enjoy the real life you have here on earth. What a bunch of deluded suckers!

But think about it for a moment from a different point of view. Let's assume religious faith *is* a fantasy. Let's assume the secular humanist evolutionary philosophy is correct: life appeared on earth by accident, there is no meaning to it at all, and once we die we cease to exist. If this view it true, then, ultimately, who cares? What difference does anything make? If there is no meaning to life, then what difference does it make whether someone spends his short, meaningless life-span clawing up the corporate ladder, or getting drunk, or watching cable TV, or accumulating sexual conquests, or deluding himself with ideas of religion? From this point of view, can anything we do today possibly affect us a hundred years from now? Of course not; we will have ceased to exist.

So, what I'm trying to say is that if my faith in God and eternity is wrong, then there is no right or wrong anyway. If my faith is a fantasy, then this is simply the activity I've chosen to pass the time during this meaningless and brief existence. It's no different than the other activities people choose to pass the time: sex, drugs, rock n' roll, shopping malls, gossip, Nintendo, sleeping, whatever.

But, if my faith in God and eternity is true...

Well, then that changes everything, doesn't it? So, to use one more Bible reference from the book of Joshua: "But as for me and my household, we will serve the Lord" (Joshua 24:15).

In conclusion, if you see me moping around and fretting too much about this or that, remind me of what I've written here. Ask me what happened to that "James Bond" confidence. I promise I won't slug you. And one other thing: when it comes time for my funeral, I don't want any weeping or hand-wringing, understand? Save the tears and the flowers for some other occasion and have a graduation party instead. And remember to put a diploma in my casket.

THE END

(WELL, ACTUALLY, IT'S MORE LIKE
THE BEGINNING!)

ENDNOTES

Chapter 4 - SCIENCE ANSWERS ALL

1. John P. Koster, Jr., *The Atheist Syndrome* (Brentwood, TN: Wolgemuth & Hyatt, Publishers, Inc. 1989) pgs. 16, 17, 27.

2. Charles Darwin, *On the Origin of Species,* 2nd. ed. (London: John Murray, 1860), pg. 481.

3. Francis Crick, *Life Itself* (New York: Simon and Schuster, 1981), pg. 88.

Chapter 7 - SEX AND DRUGS AND ROCK N' ROLL

1. I have been unable to locate the title and author of this lyric, and thus, I am unable at this time to give credit to whom it is rightly due. On the other hand, I may have simply hallucinated the song, considering how stoned I was most of the time back in those days. Either way, the words and the tune are indelibly etched in my mind.

2. Quoted by Suzanne Fields, "Sexual revolution hits a dead end," *Conservative Chronicle* (February 1, 1995) pg. 28.

Chapter 12 - CONVERSION COMPLETED

1. Jamie Buckingham, *Power for Living,* (Arthur S. DeMoss Foundation, 1984).

2. The Four Spiritual Laws and the Sinners Prayer by Bill Bright, Campus Crusade for Christ, Inc. (San Bernadino, CA, 1965).

Chapter 13 - IS THIS LOGICAL?

1. W.E. Scott, *Jesus Christ...Super-Nut? or Super-Natural!* (Glendale, CA: Dolores Press, Inc. 1972) Volumes II and III.

Chapter 14 - WOW! THERE IS NO OTHER CONCLUSION

1. Scott, *Jesus Christ...* Volume V.

2. Josh McDowell, *The Resurrection Factor,* (San Bernadino, CA: Here's Life Publishers, Inc., 1989) pg. 26.

3. Scott, *Jesus Christ...* Volumes V and VI.

4. Ibid., Volume VI.

Chapter 16 - TIME — A DIFFERENT PERSPECTIVE

1. C.S. Lewis, *Surprised by Joy,* (New York: Harcourt Brace & Company, 1955) pg. 201.

Chapter 17 - POLITICS

1. For years I've been under the impression that this quote originated in the brilliant mind of Sir Winston Churchill. But just recently I heard film critic Michael Medved say on a radio program that Otto Von Bismarck uttered a very similar expression years earlier. It being such an obvious truth about human nature, however, suffice to say that many people have drawn the same conclusion, some of whom were actually bold enough to speak aloud such a politically incorrect idea.

2. Charles Colson, *A Dance with Deception,* (Dallas: Word Publishing, 1993) pg. 23.

3. Ibid., pg. 142.

4. Ibid., pgs. 123-124.

5. Saul K. Padover, *The Washington Papers,* (New York: Harper & Brothers Publishers, 1955) pgs. 264-265.

Chapter 18 - NOT AFRAID OF DEATH

1. Bible Illustrator, (Hiawatha, IA: Parsons Technology, Inc., 1990-1992) Index 1225, no. 3/1992.3.

2. Ibid., Index 1225, no. 11/1988.3.

To order additional copies of

Boomer Trek

please send $9.99
plus $3.95 shipping and handling to:

Bill Dunn
131 Circle Drive
Torrington, CT 06790

or to order by phone,
have your credit card ready and call

1-800-917-BOOK

*Quantity Discounts are Available